SOCIAL NARRATIVES

SOCIAL NARRATIVES

A Story Intervention for
Children with Autism and
Other Developmental Disabilities

Sonia Morris

Jessica Kingsley *Publishers*
London and Philadelphia

First published in 2015
by Jessica Kingsley Publishers
73 Collier Street
London N1 9BE, UK
and
400 Market Street, Suite 400
Philadelphia, PA 19106, USA

www.jkp.com

Library of Congress Cataloging in Publication Data
Morris, Sonia, 1987-
  Social narratives : a story intervention for children with autism and other developmental disabilities / Sonia Morris.
      pages cm
  Includes bibliographical references.
  ISBN 978-1-84905-592-5 (alk. paper)
  1. Autism spectrum disorders in children--Treatment. 2. Autism spectrum disorders--Treatment. 3. Interpersonal relations. I. Title.
  RC553.A88M6787 2015
  618.92'85882--dc23
                                        2015008796

British Library Cataloguing in Publication Data
A CIP catalogue record for this book is available from the British Library

ISBN 978 1 84905 592 5
eISBN 978 1 78450 048 1

Printed and bound in Great Britain

Contents

Acknowledgements

This book has resulted from work undertaken at Trinity College Dublin while I was completing my PhD research. I would like to sincerely thank Dr Maeve Bracken for her support, encouragement and supervision during this time. Huge thanks are due to all the parents, teachers and school staff for their participation. Without you my research would not have been possible, and *Social Narratives* would never have come about. I would especially like to thank the children on the autism spectrum and their friends. They made every day different and always enjoyable. I would also like to thank my family for their love, patience and support.

Preface

My first experience with autism was when I was hired as an undergraduate student to provide respite to the family of a young girl with low functioning autistic disorder (as it was then known). I had the pleasure of working with this individual for over six years, and watched her grow from a child into a young woman. Her happiness and quirky sense of humour meant she was a joy to work with.

Despite all her gifts and endearing qualities, her social skills difficulties were apparent. She would regularly become anxious in social situations, waving her hands in the air, and hopping from one foot to the other as a method of coping. She would often blurt out inappropriate things, or bewilder other children with her unusual behaviour.

On a visit to her school one day, I met with her teacher who was looking at ways to improve her social skills. Her teacher was using written scripts to explain appropriate behaviour. She responded well to them, and I also started to write stories for her to explain other behaviours, and to motivate her to develop other skills. When the opportunity arose for me to study the merit of story interventions for children on the autism spectrum, I jumped at the chance.

While carrying out my PhD research, I noticed that there were a number of similarities between the stories teachers across Ireland were using with children on the autism spectrum. I also became more aware of how theories of autism and the learning characteristics of this population could inform the development of a standardized intervention to improve social skills. From this research, *Social Narratives* came about.

This book is an introductory guide to provide parents, teachers and caregivers instruction on how to develop and use *Social Narratives* to encourage the social skill development of children with developmental disabilities. This unique intervention places an emphasis on teaching the child how to identify potential social situations, how to go about behaving in this social situation, and what the outcome of this behaviour will be.

Once you start using *Social Narratives*, you will begin to see their potential in helping children with a myriad of social dilemmas. By writing stories, it is hoped that you will also start to see the world through the eyes of the child. You may better understand the purpose of their behaviour, how children view themselves, how they learn, and how our behaviour and environment affects them. This book will outline what *Social Narratives* are, how they are grounded in theory and research, and how to develop and implement them. My experience of using *Social Narratives* suggests that they are a useful tool for working with children with developmental disorders to improve their social skills. I hope you find them a useful and enjoyable way of teaching appropriate social behaviour.

1

What Are Social Narratives and Who Are They For?

What are Social Narratives?

Characteristics of autism spectrum disorders (ASD) manifest uniquely as a collection of symptoms that are rarely the same for any two individuals (Sansosti and Powell-Smith 2008). However, there are certain distinctive qualities that are believed to be central to a diagnosis of ASD, including deficiencies in social functioning, difficulties in the development of communication, and repetitive behaviour with an unusual strong and narrow range of interests (Baron-Cohen 2008).

Social difficulties are common to all individuals across the autism spectrum, and have been identified as the single most useful predictor of diagnostic status (Siegel *et al.* 1989). Some social skills are unaffected while others remain significantly impaired. Social difficulties for those with autism can include an extreme lack of interest in other people, unusual or absent social speech, atypical eye contact, lack of reciprocity (turn-taking), preference for being alone, difficulty determining how others feel and think, difficulty knowing how to appropriately respond to others' behaviour, inability to read emotion in the face, unusual voice or posture, and difficulty accepting that there are other perspectives rather than a single correct perspective (Baron-Cohen 2008; Carter *et al.* 2005).

As a consequence of these deficits, those on the autism spectrum tend not to initiate social interaction or play cooperatively with peers (Hauck *et al.* 1995; Kokina and Kern 2010; Quirmbach *et al.* 2009). Some individuals withdraw entirely from social interactions, while those who search for social contact have interactions that are awkward or inappropriate (Beauchamp and Anderson 2010).

Language and communication impairments are closely linked to the deficits in social functioning observed in ASD (Järvinen-Pasley *et al.* 2008). Those on the autism spectrum demonstrate a restricted range of social communication skills such as difficulty initiating and maintaining conversations, listening and responding to peers and adults, and interacting in basic games (Sansosti and Powell-Smith 2008). These individuals often find it difficult to communicate their needs and desires. Related to this, communicative functions such as making requests, commenting on things, asking questions, protesting and negotiating are often absent or abnormal. As a consequence, in social exchanges, those with ASD find it difficult to know what information to convey, often saying and doing things that others construe as inappropriate.

Reports suggest that the number of children diagnosed with ASD has been rising in recent years, so much so that it is considered the fastest growing developmental disability (Sansosti and Powell-Smith 2008). The most recent prevalence estimates suggest that autism affects one in every 68 individuals, one in every 42 boys and one in every 189 girls (Centers for Disease Control and Prevention 2014). With a growing number of individuals on the autism spectrum, there is a need to develop interventions that improve social competence and quality of life. One such intervention is Social Narratives.

Social Narratives are short stories that address the social deficits that characterize ASD. They were designed as a tool to educate an individual on social behaviour relevant to them, and to motivate them to perform this behaviour when appropriate. These stories can be used to target new behaviours that the child has never displayed previously, and also to increase the frequency of behaviours the child has demonstrated in the past but that are inconsistently used.

The aim of the story is to explain behaviour. Children with developmental delay, and in particular those on the autism spectrum, may find certain social situations difficult to understand. They may not know why people behave the way they do, and how to behave and respond in turn. Social Narratives explain how to recognize when it is appropriate to display a particular social behaviour, for example, when eating lunch as part of a group, when playing on the playground, or after a social prompt from a playmate. This intervention also provides suggestions of appropriate behaviours in particular social situations, why that behaviour is suitable, and how it influences others.

Social Narratives also have a secondary function. Research has suggested that anxiety disorders affect between 30 and 80 per cent of children on the autism spectrum (Muris *et al.* 1998; Wood *et al.* 2009). Social Narratives attempt to lower the levels of anxiety experienced by children with social difficulties in social situations, by acting as a priming strategy. They may reduce levels of stress and anxiety by preparing the child for what is ahead. The stories also reassure the child that certain behaviours are okay, their emotional reactions and feelings are okay, and people's expectations are okay. For example, a Social Narrative might reassure a child that it is acceptable to like certain cartoons and to talk about them even if others do not share this interest, but at the same time, the story encourages the child to talk about a variety of things with other children, and not to just focus on one topic of interest.

Social Narratives are an adult-led intervention. This means that those who know the child best develop the stories. This includes the child's caregivers, whether it is a parent, teacher, special needs assistant, child-minder or professional. The stories are easy to develop by design and not time-consuming. Once written, the intervention should take less than five minutes a day to implement.

The Social Narrative intervention was developed based on the cognitive and learning characteristics of those with ASD. Chapters 2 and 3 of this book outline three major theories of autism, and how Social Narratives were developed with these theories in mind. Chapter 4 outlines how to write Social Narratives in a number of easy-to-follow steps, while Chapter 5 explains the implementation process. Social Narrative interventions have also been tested to investigate if they are effective with an autism population at increasing pro-social behaviour. Chapter 6 summarizes these findings, and also presents feedback, both from children who received this intervention and those who developed and implemented them. In the final chapter of this book, a number of sample stories are provided. Please feel free to copy and tailor these stories for your own needs.

Who is best suited to receiving a Social Narrative intervention?

Before reading any further, it is a good idea to make sure that this intervention is suitable for the individual you are working with. The good news is that almost all children can benefit from Social Narratives. This intervention is centred on children's familiarity with storybooks. Social Narratives explain social interactions with the ultimate aim of increasing understanding, improving social competence and improving relationships with peers and siblings. This intervention is, of course, better suited to some children than others.

Social Narratives are a verbal intervention, so comprehension of the verbal information used is vital for the child to internalize the message, and to adopt the desired behaviour. Success of the intervention is therefore increased with improved verbal ability, and verbal comprehension in particular. Bear in mind, however, that older children with advanced verbal skills may not be suited to receiving Social Narratives. They could easily view the format and structure of a Social Narrative as condescending, with their advanced abilities. Children over 13 years of age attending an integrated school setting may benefit more from a different form of social skills intervention, such as drama classes or social skills groups that include elements of modelling and role-play.

There is also no point learning a new social behaviour if there is no one with whom to practice the newly acquired skill. It is imperative that the children receiving Social Narrative interventions have access to a social environment. They should be provided with the opportunity to display the targeted behaviour by having regular access to appropriate peers. For example, teachers considering using Social Narratives with a particular child should consider the educational setting. A child educated in school on a one-to-one basis with no access to play partners is unlikely to benefit from this intervention. Similarly, parents thinking of using Social Narratives with their child should make sure that the child has access to play partners such as siblings or other children outside of school. If no suitable peers are readily or consistently available, parents should contact the child's teacher and get them involved in the intervention too.

Social Narratives were developed with the unique qualities of ASD in mind. The clinical definition of autism has loosened in recent years. The diagnostic categories of autistic disorder, Asperger's syndrome and pervasive developmental disorders not otherwise specified have recently been combined to make the autism spectrum disorder. Thus, autism is currently viewed as a spectrum disorder with various classifications of severity. When developed correctly, Social Narratives can be successful with children across the spectrum.

Social Narratives are used to develop useful social skills. The social difficulties observed in ASD are not unique to this condition, however. Social Narratives may also prove a useful learning tool for those with a variety of alternative diagnoses, including those with attention deficit hyperactivity disorder (ADHD) and learning disability. Even typical children with social difficulties can benefit from a Social Narrative intervention.

The next chapter provides a brief overview of the three prominent theories of ASD: theory of mind deficits, executive dysfunction and weak central coherence. These three theories are linked to the social skills deficits that those on the spectrum commonly display.

2

Theories of Autism
Spectrum Disorders

When developing an intervention for children on the autism spectrum, it is not only important to know the behavioural traits associated with autism, but also why these traits exist. Understanding the nature of the cognitive processes underlying the core deficits of autism has recently been the focus of much research. A consistent finding is that there are indeed differences in the structure of the autistic brain when compared to those without ASD, and there are also apparent differences in brain functioning. For example, areas normally associated with social behaviour are under-active in the brains of those with ASD (Baron-Cohen 2008).

Advances in technology have made it possible to investigate the relationship between brain structure and functioning underlying the behavioural traits of autism. Studies suggest, however, that a single underlying feature of the autistic brain is unlikely to account for all the clinical features of ASD (Juranek *et al.* 2006). The theories put forward to explain ASD mostly point to impairments in attention, information processing and memory (Quill 1997). There are three major theories of ASD – theory of mind, executive dysfunction and weak central coherence – which are now discussed in turn, with a particular emphasis on how they impact social functioning.

Theory of mind

The first theory of ASD discussed in this chapter is theory of mind. Successful negotiation of the social world requires an understanding of the beliefs, intentions, feelings and desires of others. Theory of mind is the ability to realize that other people have mental states, and that these mental states are different to one's own. The theory of mind model suggests that those with ASD either do not develop theory of mind, or have a significant delay in acquiring this ability (Baron-Cohen 1988). A deficit in theory of mind makes it difficult to recognize and accurately interpret the emotions, intentions and behaviours of others (White *et al.* 2010). This can make it difficult for children with ASD to engage in appropriate social behaviour.

Theory of mind usually develops in a relatively stable and predictable sequence. A typical 14-month-old child shows what is called 'joint attention'. This allows the child to orient and attend to a social partner, to read and share emotional states, and to establish and follow attentional focus in social interactions. Thus, joint attention is necessary for social problem-solving and judgement. Joint attention is considered a precursor to theory of mind as it underlies the capacity to understand the thoughts and intentions of others (Beauchamp and Anderson 2010). While most of those on the autism spectrum do show some aspects of joint attention, the amount of time engaged in joint attention is reduced.

By the age of two, children usually begin to engage in symbolic play, which involves some aspects of theory of mind. Interacting with those who are pretending requires mind-reading skills to understand that in the other person's mind they are just pretending. Studies have suggested that most children with ASD show less pretend play, and the play that is displayed is limited to rule-based formats (Baron-Cohen 2008).

By the age of three, there is usually an understanding that there are differences between personal mental states and others. Thus, typical three-year-olds can pass the 'seeing leads to knowing' test. To pass the test, the child must realize that touching a box does not mean someone knows what is in the box. They must recognize that seeing is the only way to gain this knowledge. Most children on the autism spectrum are delayed in passing this test (Baron-Cohen and Goodhart 1994).

By the age of four, children usually pass false belief tasks, and it is on these tasks that most of the theory of mind research with ASD has been based. The Sally Anne false belief test is one of the more popular tests of theory of mind. It involves two dolls, one called Sally and the other called Anne. First, an adult shows the child the doll called Sally. The adult tells the child that Sally hides a marble in a box. The Sally doll is seen to pick up the marble and put it in a box. The adult then removes the Sally doll from view. The doll called Anne is then introduced to the child. The Adult tells the child that while Sally is out, Anne moves the marble to the basket. The Anne doll is seen to remove the marble from the box and place it in the basket. To pass the test, the child must recognize that, when the Sally doll returns, she will still look for her marble in the box even though it is not there. Most children on the autism spectrum will say that Sally will look for the marble where it actually is. In this way, they fail to consider another person's point of view (Baron-Cohen, Leslie and Frith 1985).

Studies also suggest that some children with ASD are delayed in developing understanding for second-order mind-reading (Baron-Cohen *et al.* 1999), in recognizing what hurts another's feelings and what might be better left unspoken (Baron-Cohen 2008), in predicting emotion based on a person's belief, and in matching different modes of emotional expression, such as facial expressions, vocalizations and gestures (Silver and Oakes 2001).

Theory of mind deficits can account for the difficulties those with ASD have in social situations. It can explain why those with autism may fail to act appropriately for their age in social situations, and may be unable to reciprocate in social interactions or participate in cooperative play.

Executive dysfunction

Executive function is the ability to control action. This includes the ability to plan ahead and to make behavioural goals, to control one's own attention processes, and to generate novel behaviours (Rutherford and Rogers 2003). The theory of executive dysfunction suggests that the core features of ASD are best explained by an inability to plan action and to shift attention (Hughes, Russell and Robbins 1994).

Individuals with ASD may display behavioural excesses that can also interfere with their social relationships. Compared to their peers, children on the autism spectrum engage in higher rates of repetitive and self-injurious behaviour (McConnell 2002). Repetitive and restrictive behaviours in children with autism can manifest in many ways, from simple sensori-motor actions (e.g. hand flapping, spinning, lining things up, and a need for sameness) to a complex narrow ranges of interests (Chen, Rodgers and McConachie 2009). These restrictive, repetitive and stereotyped patterns of behaviour, coupled with communication difficulties, can create significant problems for engagement in typical social interactions, often resulting in avoidance of social contacts, over-arousal in social situations, confusion over social rules and expectations, and social rejection (Cotugno 2009).

The theory of executive dysfunction helps explain the repetitive behaviours observed in those with ASD as an inability to move flexibly from one behaviour to another. This theory can also explain the deficits in social functioning common to those on the autism spectrum. Executive functioning is needed to self-monitor behaviour in social situations. It allows someone to recognize when a behaviour could be socially inappropriate, and to inhibit that behaviour. Furthermore, to communicate effectively in a conversation, an individual is required to stay on task and recognize the beginning, middle and end of an interaction, to interpret the speech and body language information provided by others in the conversation, to decide what information is important to the conversation and which is not important, and to make sure that their own responses and body language are appropriate (Bartak, Bottroff and Zeitz 2006). This could prove very difficult for those with impairments in executive functioning.

Studies suggest that problems in executive functioning are often present in patients with brain damage, particularly damage to the prefrontal cortex. While those with ASD do not have any obvious damage to their frontal lobes, the theory proposes that the prefrontal cortex may develop differently in this population. In support of this theory, children on the autism spectrum do show deficits in a variety of executive function tasks (Hughes *et al.* 1994; Russell *et al.* 1991).

A limitation of this theory is that it presumes the narrow interests in autism reflect an inability to shift attention to new topics. This completely ignores the content of these interests, which is far from random. It cannot explain why a large number of children on the autism spectrum find similar topics, such as numbers or objects (such as trains), interesting and motivating.

Weak central coherence

The last major theory of autism discussed is weak central coherence. This theory suggests that the behavioural differences observed in autism spectrum disorders are due to a tendency to see only small details and an inability to see the bigger picture, which is necessary for interpreting social information. When an individual interacts with the environment, they tend to recall an overall impression of that interaction, or the 'gist' of what has happened. For example, if asked to complete the sentence 'Go hunting with a knife and…', most people would say something like '…catch a bear'. Those on the autism spectrum have a tendency to focus too much on the small details at the expense of understanding actual meaning or considering the context. They may complete the sentence 'Go hunting with a knife and…' with the word 'fork' (Booth and Happé 2010).

This theory offers an explanation for some of the many positive features of autism, such as excellent attention to, and memory for, detail and skills in a specific topic. This theory can also explain why skills such as recognizing facial expressions may be absent or impaired in individuals with ASD (Carter *et al.* 2005). Those with autism may just focus on the mouth rather than what the whole face is expressing.

However, weak central coherence is not common to all individuals on the autism spectrum (Burnette *et al.* 2005). For those on the autism spectrum who do display weak central coherence, this can be used to explain some of the difficulties these individuals have in social situations. It is possible that those with ASD may pay more attention to irrelevant details in a social situation, and so fail to grasp the meaning of social exchanges (Kokina and Kern 2010). This can lead to impairment in social functioning.

In the next chapter, theory of mind, executive dysfunction and weak central coherence are applied to the development of Social Narrative interventions. The chapter then explains how a Social Narrative may go about improving social skills based on the learning and cognitive characteristics of children with ASD.

3

Applying Theory to Social Narratives

Social Narratives address several areas of preference and relative strength in those with ASD. They share information about what could happen in the future, which addresses a need for predictability (APA 2000). The stories are read over many sessions, which also appeals to a preference for routine (APA 2000). Furthermore, they are presented in a written form, appealing to a relative strength in understanding visually presented information (Okada *et al.* 2010). The success of Social Narratives in improving the social skills of children on the autism spectrum can be further explained using the three cognitive theories outlined in the previous chapter.

Theory of mind

As outlined in Chapter 2, the theory of mind account emphasizes the difficulties many individuals with ASD have in relation to emotion perception, attributing thoughts and feelings to others, taking the perspective of others, understanding that others have different beliefs and intentions, and interpreting the behaviours of others (Baron-Cohen 2008; Loth, Gómez and Happé 2008). Social Narratives may be effective at increasing the social behaviour of those on the autism spectrum by helping compensate for these deficits, by providing the information that is missing as a consequence of impaired theory of mind.

Theory of mind deficits make it difficult to intuitively define, understand and interpret what is likely to happen in a social situation. They are a priming strategy, allowing an individual to preview information, which in turn increases social competence (Koegel *et al.* 2003). The aim is to increase the understanding and predictability of the social situation. Social Narratives provide accurate information regarding the who, what, when and where of a social situation. This can help explain the intentions of others. An example is a story that focuses on encouraging a child to respond to questions asked by peers. The story can explain why the questions are asked in the first place – for example, to start a conversation, or to make friends. This can help the child understand the behaviours of others. The story can also be used to explain in explicit terms the social behaviour expected of them in particular social situations, and suggestions on how to go about performing this behaviour. Furthermore, Social Narratives explain how this behaviour will make people feel, compensating for an impairment in interpreting the emotions of others.

Executive dysfunction

Executive dysfunction results in impairments in planning, organization, flexibility and self-regulation (Ozonoff 1998). Executive processes can be seen to be goal-directed and future-orientated. Read in advance of the social situation, story interventions increase the predictability of the situation, and explicitly explain what behaviour is expected. Social Narratives provide a social plan, or plan of action, that can be applied across many social contexts. The stories may achieve behavioural change by giving examples of specific social cues and behaviours. This may lead to improvement in social problem-solving. Social Narratives help children make the link between a particular cue in their environment, like playtime in the classroom, and a particular social behaviour, like joining in play with classmates. Therefore, Social Narrative interventions could compensate for impairments in these areas by helping those with ASD plan future social interactions.

Furthermore, because the same story is read every day, those with ASD has access to concrete and consistent information which may reduce the need to hold information in working memory, reducing cognitive load, and facilitate self-monitoring (Reynhout and Carter 2011).

As a consequence of executive dysfunction, individuals on the autism spectrum may find it difficult to generate words that are relevant to a social context or topic. This theory can also explain why those with ASD may be unable to generate novel responses without prompting (Lopez *et al.* 2005). Children on the autism spectrum may recognize social cues in the environment, and may be aware that they are supposed to do something, but find it difficult to decipher what that something is. It has been suggested that exemplars of what to say and do may be necessary for interventions targeting social behaviour to be successful (Kenworthy *et al.* 2009). This may explain why Social Narratives, which include plenty of suggestions of how to perform a targeted social behaviour, are successful at teaching new social skills.

The presentation of repetitive behaviours in ASD has also been linked to executive dysfunction (Boyd *et al.* 2009; Kenworthy *et al.* 2009; LeMonda, Holtzer and Goldman 2012; Lopez *et al.* 2005; Sayers *et al.* 2011). It is hypothesized that executive dysfunction results in an individual being unable to plan and control behaviour, including the ability to inhibit an ongoing response, or to spontaneously generate a new one. Thus, in the absence of an alternative behaviour, children with autism may engage in repetitive behaviour. By providing appropriate responses for a given situation, Social Narrative interventions may change behaviour by helping suppress automatic and incorrect responses (Reynhout and Carter 2011).

Weak central coherence

Social information needs to be interpreted in context in order to comprehend the meaning of the social interaction and to respond appropriately (Begeer *et al.* 2010). The diminished ability of those with ASD to separate the important details in a social situation from the irrelevant details (weak central coherence) could also be ameliorated using Social Narrative interventions by helping focus the individual's attention on relevant information.

Social Narratives are written to explain the meaning of complex social situations. They also emphasize the relevant details needed for appropriate behaviour. Access to this information prior to the social situation may help the individual better understand the situation and prepare accordingly (Reynhout and Carter 2011). Furthermore, story interventions are a form of social script that provides descriptions of the environment and instructions on how to behave appropriately, which could be considered rules for social situations. Rule-driven social interactions mean that strong central coherence is no longer essential for an appropriate response (Begeer *et al.* 2010).

In conclusion, different elements of Social Narrative interventions may compensate for different cognitive deficits in ASD. The stories are written in such a way as to provide explanations of the social environment to increase predictability and to explain the perspectives of others that may compensate for impaired theory of mind. By providing an explicit plan of action of what to do in specific social situations, executive dysfunction could be ameliorated. Furthermore, weak central coherence could be compensated for using Social Narratives, which emphasize the important details in social situations, and provide a set of rules for social engagements.

The next chapter is a practical guide to writing your own Social Narrative interventions presented in ten easy-to-follow steps.

4

Writing a Social Narrative

So now you know what a Social Narrative is, and you are ready to start writing some stories. The steps to writing your own stories are outlined below. Use the checklist provided in Chapter 7 to make sure your stories meet all the criteria for a Social Narrative. You can also refer to the sample stories provided in Chapter 8 as inspiration, or to check that you are on the right track.

Step 1: Identifying a behaviour to target

Identifying a behaviour to target can often be the hardest step. The child in question may have many social difficulties, and knowing where to start can be tough. It can be difficult to pick a single skill to target. Observing the child during free playtime at home, in the classroom, and on the playground is a good starting point. Compare the child's behaviour to that of their siblings or classmates to identify where the child is having the most difficulty. Discuss your findings with the child's parents and teachers for their input. Always remember that a child's behaviour at school can be different from their behaviour at home. For more advanced children, you might consider asking for their input into story development. Do they have any social behaviours that they find confusing and want explained?

Behaviours you may consider targeting include:

» Greetings (saying hello, waving)

» Conversational skills (joining in conversations, starting conversations, sharing interests, taking turns in conversations)

» Joining in play

» Game playing skills (following the rules of the game, taking turns, being a good winner or loser, sharing)

» Teaching social skills for new situations (birthday parties, the park).

You should now have a list of social behaviours that the child is having difficulty with. Review this list and rank the behaviours in order of difficulty. Select a behaviour that is within the child's learning capabilities. If the child has never engaged in social communication, then a story aimed at encouraging reciprocal conversations is too advanced. Start small and target something like social greetings or initiating conversation.

Ask yourself if the behaviour you have chosen can be broken down further into smaller more manageable behaviours. For example, if you have noted that the child has difficulty engaging in cooperative play, look at what behaviours are present in cooperative play. You could first encourage the child to engage in parallel play where they merely play within the proximity of their peers. After the child is comfortable with this, sharing could be targeted and the child could be encouraged to play with the same toy as their peers. Following mastery of this skill, a story could then be created to encourage the child to play cooperatively with the other children.

A good way to check and see if the behaviour chosen is too complicated is to look at the sentences used in the story to instruct their behaviour. Is each sentence a variant of the target behaviour? Or is each one targeting a separate behaviour? A story with sentences like 'I will try to sit beside my classmates during free time', 'I will try to share my toys with my classmates', and 'I will try to play a game with my classmates with the toys' may overload the child. For some children, keeping it simple will result in greater success.

Once you have decided on a behaviour to target, you can write the title of the story. This should include the social behaviour to be learned and the child's name so that the child knows that it is their story. An example of a Social Narrative title is 'Sharing toys with my sister – Peter's story'.

Top Tip: Preliminary research suggests that story interventions with the aim of teaching a child a new skill are more effective than stories attempting to increase the frequency of skills the child already knows.

Step 2: Checking for negative behaviours

Related to Step 1 above, the target behaviour should have a positive focus rather than a negative focus. The purpose of a Social Narrative is to encourage children to learn a new social skill. Focusing on a new skill can be difficult if the biggest problem the child is having is that negative behaviours are interfering with successful social interactions. For example, a child may enjoy playing with Lego® during free time at school, with little regard for their play partners' choice of games. This could discourage children from engaging in future exchanges with the child. It may be tempting to write a story encouraging the child to stop choosing Lego® to play with when they are with their classmates. The issue with this approach, however, is that you are stopping the child from doing something that they are familiar and feel comfortable with, and offering no alternative to this behaviour. The child should understand that there is nothing wrong with playing with what they enjoy, but they should also understand that others may not share this interest. Rather than a story focusing on preventing the child from playing with Lego, the story should focus on encouraging the child to ask their play partner about what they like to play with, and to take turns choosing games.

Step 3: Gathering information about the child

The behaviour to be targeted has been decided. The next step in the process is to gather the information needed to write the story. This includes the child's reading level, interests and daily schedule.

It is important that the story is tailored to the reading abilities of the child. A story that is too long and complicated will discourage the child from reading it on a regular basis, and may obscure the lesson of the story. Likewise, a story that is too short and easy may be condescending to more advanced readers. Parents writing the story for a child should ask the child's teacher to review the story. The story should take about five minutes to read, if it is tailored correctly.

It is important to include the child's interests in the story. This is elaborated on further in Step 7 below. The simplest way to find out these interests is to ask the child directly.

Interests could be anything from their favourite food, favourite cartoon character, or favourite subject.

Finally, the story should tell the child when it is appropriate to perform the targeted behaviour. Remember that those with autism are literal thinkers. If the story does not explicitly state when behaviour is to be performed, the child is likely to perform it at inappropriate times. Periods during the child's daily schedule when the behaviour is expected to occur must be identified. For teachers, the social behaviour targeted is more than likely appropriate during lunch or playtime at school. For parents writing a story to be used at home, appropriate times are likely to be when the child is with their siblings, in a playground or in a social group.

Step 4: Starting to write the story – what sentences can I use?

It is time to put pen to paper. Have a look at the sample stories included in this book in Chapter 8 for inspiration. The easiest way to start the story is with a simple sentence like 'My name is Sonia.' This sentence lets the child know immediately that the story is relevant to them, and that it is their story.

This sentence type is called a *factual sentence*. It is merely a statement of what is true, or what is believed to be true. There are three different types of factual sentences that are used to create a Social Narrative. The first, *setting sentences*, aims to increase the child's understanding of social situations, and are used to describe:

- » Who the child is, for example, 'My name is Sonia.'

- » What the child likes to do, or their interests, for example, 'I like to play with trains.'

- » When the target behaviour is expected to occur, for example, 'After eating my lunch, I usually have playtime at school.'

- » Where the target behaviour is expected to occur, for example, 'Sometimes I play in the playground.'

These sentences can also describe information about other people, and not just the child, for example, 'Most children join in games at playtime.' They could also refer to a cultural belief or principle, for example, 'It does not matter who wins or loses in games', or a factual statement, for example, 'There are ten people in my class.'

The next type of sentence in this category is referred to as *reassuring sentences*. These aim to lower the anxiety of the child and to promote positive self-esteem. When writing a Social Narrative, it is important that the child is not criticized. For example, when talking with their peers, some children with autism have a tendency to talk at length about their special interests. They may interrupt conversation on a topic that does not interest them in favour of one that does. As a consequence, the conversation can often be very one-sided, with the child showing little regard for conversational partners. A Social Narrative aimed at joining in conversations that discourages the child from talking about their interests, or that suggests that their interests are in any way a bad thing, may increase anxiety for that child. Instead, it is preferable to suggest alternative behaviours and to explain the benefits of these new behaviours. It is also important to reassure the child that their interests and feelings are normal and acceptable. Reassurance sentences fulfil this role, most often following a setting sentence, for example, 'Sometimes I talk about trains and how they work. This is okay', or 'Different people have different interests. This is okay.' This type of sentence can also follow a sentence instructing behaviour to reinforce the benefit of that behaviour, for example, 'I will try to join in games with my friends. This is a good thing to do.'

The last type of factual sentence is concerned with providing information the child on the autism spectrum may be lacking as a consequence of theory of mind deficits. These are called *theory of mind sentences*. These explain others' actions/expectations and the emotions of others, for example, 'My friends will be happy if I play with them at lunchtime', or 'Children play games together at lunchtime because they think it is fun.' Theory of mind sentences are usually used to explain the perspectives of others, and not the child receiving the story. It is important not to assume the child's feelings in case your assumptions are wrong. If you do infer the child's mental state in a story, make sure that it is done in a general way, and not definitively. For example, you may have noticed that when the child is playing a game with other children, they can be overly rule-orientated. They may insist that other children abide by their playing rules, and get upset when they do not. We might instinctively include in the story a sentence like, 'I think that my classmates are cheating.' We are assuming what the child is thinking. Instead, this sentence could be rewritten in a more general way by including words like 'sometimes', 'usually', 'may', 'might' or 'probably' – '*Sometimes* I *might* think that my classmates are cheating.'

Factual sentences are unlikely to encourage any behavioural change. A contributing factor to the social deficit in autism is an inability to voluntarily bring to mind appropriate social behaviour (Quill 1997). This means that although children on the autism spectrum may be aware of having to do something in social situations, they may have difficulty bringing appropriate behaviour to mind without direction (Quirmbach *et al.* 2009). To motivate the child to perform a targeted behaviour, *instructive sentences* are included in the story. These sentences suggest to the child appropriate behaviours in a particular social context. When the story is read just before a social situation, instructive sentences may also prime the child by explicitly stating the desired behaviour.

It is important to remember that these sentences are suggestions of appropriate behaviour, so should be phrased as 'I could' or 'I will try to' rather than as 'I will' or 'I must'. Those on the autism spectrum often interpret things literally. If phrased in a definitive way, the child may think that the behaviour can only be performed in a particular way, and the child may not feel comfortable with the suggested behaviour, causing anxiety. For example, if a Social Narrative is written to encourage a child to start conversations with their siblings and we write something like, 'I will start a conversation with my sister Lisa. I will ask her how school was today. I will ask her what her favourite cartoon is', the child may assume that these are the only options available for starting a conversation with Lisa. Poor Lisa could be asked the same two questions repeatedly every day. Instead, we might write something like, 'I will try to start a conversation with my sister Lisa. I could ask her how school was today. I could ask her what her favourite cartoon is. I could ask her something else.'

Different sentence types in Social Narratives have different functions within a story. The four sentence types used to create a Social Narrative are summarized in Table 4.1 with further examples. When all sentence types are presented together, the individual with autism has access to a coherent and whole description of the social situation.

Table 4.1: Summary of the types of sentences used
to construct a Social Narrative intervention

Type of sentence	Description of sentence	Examples
Factual setting	Statements that aim to increase understanding of social situations. These sentences answer the who, what, when and where of social situations.	• My teacher's name is Ms Phelan. • The first thing we do at school in the morning is have free time. • Children play games at free time. • During free time I sometimes play with a dinosaur.
Reassuring	Statements that aim to decrease anxiety and raise positive self-esteem. They reassure the child that certain feelings and behaviours are acceptable.	• This is okay. • Everybody feels like this sometimes. • This is a good thing to do.
Theory of mind	These statements are used to compensate for theory of mind deficits. They refer to, or describe, another's knowledge or thoughts, feelings, beliefs, opinions and motivations.	• My friends like it when I listen to them speaking about their interests. • My teacher is happy when I play nicely. • My sister knows that I like trains. • Children play together because they think it is fun.
Instructive	These are statements that describe/identify and encourage a desired response to a particular social situation.	• I will try to say hello to my classmates. • I will try to play trains with brother. • I could build a castle out of Lego® with my sister. • I could say to Simon, 'What did you do at the weekend?'

Two types of general sentences have been outlined – factual and instructive. The inclusion of too many instructive sentences in a Social Narrative, however, runs a risk of the story becoming merely a list of directions for the child to follow without any explanation as to why this is important. The inclusion of too few instructive sentences runs a risk that the child may not be motivated to perform the behaviour, or may not have enough knowledge about how to perform the behaviour. The aim of a Social Narrative is to strike the right balance between fact and instruction. It is therefore recommended that for every instructive sentence included in the story, there is also a factual sentence. This should provide the child with the knowledge of not only what to do, but also where to do it, and why they should do it.

Step 5: Writing the story from the first-person perspective

The body of a Social Narrative is written from the first-person perspective. This presents information from an individual's own vantage point, using the pronouns 'I' and 'we', for example, 'I go to the playground after school each day' or 'We eat our lunch in the classroom.' For most people, information is better remembered when it is self-relevant (Henderson *et al.* 2009; Klein 2012; Lind 2010). This is known as the self-reference effect. The presence of a self-reference effect suggests that a story describing the actions of others, for example, 'The children will try to play together', will not be remembered as well as a story with self-reference, for example, 'I will try to play with the children' (Klein 2012). Studies have suggested that children with ASD also demonstrate a self-reference effect (Lombardo *et al.* 2007). Social Narratives should therefore be written from the child's point of view.

Step 6: Checking the language used is literal and positive

Social Narratives are written using language that increases the effectiveness of the intervention. When writing your stories, it is important to make sure that the sentences used cannot be misinterpreted. Social Narratives are written as literal as possible. The reason for this is because children on the autism spectrum are known for their literal interpretation of language (Kanner 1943). Research suggests that individuals with autism remember better with language that is clear and concise (Minshew and Williams 2008). Thus, avoid confusing statements. This means that all statements that could be misinterpreted should be removed. For example, saying something like 'I will be a happy camper if I play with my friends' could be very confusing for those on the autism spectrum, who may interpret it to mean an actual camping trip is on the cards if they perform the target behaviour.

In addition to the use of literal language, a Social Narrative always uses positive language, for example, 'I will try to be quiet' rather than 'I will not shout.' There are a number of reasons for this. First, it has been reported that, in a typical population, naming a behaviour to avoid sometimes causes that behaviour to happen, for example, stuttering or movement difficulties (Donnellan *et al.* 2006). Second, providing information about what to do in a given situation, rather than what not to do, can protect a child's positive self-esteem. Self-esteem seems to be affected by self-evaluative statements – for example, 'I am smart' would raise self-esteem while 'I am stupid' would lower it (Coleman 1975). Additionally, from an autism perspective, negatives such as 'I will not run' can cause confusion (Janzen, Baron and Groden 2006). Thus, to increase understanding and appropriate behaviours, and to maintain self-esteem, Social Narrative interventions avoid the use of negative statements.

Step 7: Including the interests of the child

Your story is almost finished. We should now be thinking of how we can motivate the child to read the story from start to finish over a number of days. One way of doing this is to incorporate the child's special interests or specialist subjects into the story.

Those on the autism spectrum often demonstrate an intense focus on a narrow range of interests. You may have, or work with, a child who is mad about trains, computer games, art, Disney DVDs or robots, for example. These special interests can be highly important and meaningful to the child. Therefore, these are interests that they find motivating and reinforcing (Keeling et al. 2003). It is suggested that special interests could be effective tools in teaching behaviours that children with autism would otherwise have little motivation to learn (Campbell and Tincani 2011).

Research studies have found that the incorporation of special interests in social interventions increases initiations for social sharing (Vismara and Lyons 2007), social interaction (Baker 2000), social initiations (Boyd et al. 2007), social responding (Charlop-Christy and Haymes 1998), and focused conversation (Davis et al. 2010). Thus, it appears possible to increase a desired behaviour by capitalizing on a child's interests. Research also suggests that attention to a story can be maintained by including the interests of the child (Davis et al. 2010). Furthermore, the autism literature also suggests that by including the interests of the child, the chance that they will reject the intervention is lessened (Davis *et al.* 2010). With evidence of increased effectiveness, attention and compliance, Social Narratives should always aim to include the child's interests.

The question now is how to incorporate these interests into the story. There are a number of different ways this can be done. The first is to use the child's interests to set up the story and to confirm ownership of the story. You could start the story like, 'My name is Ross. I go to Fairview Junior School.' You could then include a setting sentence like 'My favourite toy to play with at lunch is a robot with red buttons and a blue head.'

Another option is to use the child's interests to explain the behaviour of others in certain social situations by incorporating them into theory of mind sentences. Special interests in cartoon characters or particular DVDs really lend themselves to this. For example, to explain friendships to a child who has a particular interest in Thomas the Tank Engine, you could include a sentence in the story like, 'Most children like having a friend, just like the way Thomas likes having Percy as a friend.'

Another useful way of including a child's special interests in a Social Narrative is to integrate them into instructive sentences. The interests could be used as performance options for the targeted behaviour. For example, a Social Narrative encouraging a child with an interest in sporting facts to start conversations with their peers could include sentences like, 'I could ask my friends what their favourite premiership football team is. I could then tell them who the top goal scorer of this year is for that team.' By including topics the child finds appealing in the instructive sentences, the child may have an increased motivation to engage in the targeted behaviour.

Top Tip: You may know beyond a shadow of a doubt what the child's interests are, but for those of you who are even the slightest bit unsure, the best thing to do is to ask the child outright what their favourite hobby is. Chances are they will be more than happy to talk at length about this. Alternatively, if you are working with a shy, quiet, unforthcoming or non-verbal child, observation is key. Does the child engage in the same behaviours and choose the same toys whenever they are free to play?

Step 8: Including pictures

Social Narratives use pictures to reinforce the lesson of each story. Different processes in the brain are responsible for different things. One part of the brain is responsible for encoding language, while a different process interprets visual imagery (Kana *et al.* 2006). Research strongly suggests that children on the autism spectrum are visual learners (West 2008). This means that these children may find it easier to interpret and understand information that is presented in a written or picture form than information that they hear without any visual support. It is widely agreed that the use of visual supports, and visual methods of teaching, are, for many children on the autism spectrum, effective intervention strategies (O'Connor 2009).

Social Narratives, presented in book format with all the information written clearly and concisely, appeal to the learning characteristics of those on the autism spectrum. Pictures can further the effectiveness of Social Narratives by helping to make this information more meaningful. Pictures will help children further understand the meaning of the story (Kana *et al.* 2006; Mesibov and Howley 2003). Thus, Social Narratives should always include illustrations to aid comprehension and an increased rate of learning.

There are many different types of illustrations that could be incorporated into a Social Narrative, including photographs, drawings, clipart, emoticons, figures and charts. Photographs can be particularly useful for supporting setting sentences. A photograph of the child could be included to further reinforce the idea of the child owning the story. A photograph of where the targeted social behaviour is expected to occur, like the playground, the classroom, the sports hall etc., is also an excellent way of eliminating any confusion as to exactly where this behaviour should be performed. Even a photograph of the child's social partners can help explain with whom the child should be engaging.

Emoticons are great for supporting both theory of mind and reassuring sentences. They can be used to demonstrate the emotions of others, for example, a large happy face to support the sentence 'My friends will be happy if I ask them about their interests.' Similarly, they can be used to comfort the child, for example, a picture of a smiley face with thumbs up could support the sentences 'I will try to share my toys with my brother. This is a good thing to do.'

Drawings can be used to demonstrate new behaviours that the child has yet to master. For example, if the Social Narrative is targeting cooperative play, a picture of children sitting together and playing a single game should explain to the child what is meant by the term 'playing together'. Getting the child to draw their own pictures for inclusion in the story is also a fun activity, and engages the child in the Social Narrative.

Top Tip: Why not include a picture of the child's interests in the story too? For example, a child with a love of Thomas the Tank Engine may enjoy having a smiley Thomas face rather than a standard emoticon.

Step 9: Writing comprehension questions

Using a comprehension question can be useful when introducing new concepts, like a new behaviour to learn using a Social Narrative. Comprehension is often impaired in those on the autism spectrum. Even though a child may be capable of speaking in complex sentences, they may not comprehend what they have spoken (Minshew and Williams 2008). A possible procedure to motivate children with autism to attend to the information presented in a Social Narrative is to ask comprehension questions after the story has been read. If comprehension is persistently low, the story could be reviewed to aid understanding. Thus, Social Narratives always have comprehension questions to assess understanding.

Comprehension questions should be written on a separate page at the end of the story. Three comprehension questions are optimal per story. Social Narratives are short, so there shouldn't be too many questions to ask. The three questions should address knowledge of a setting question (e.g. 'Who can I play with in the playground?'), an instructive question (e.g. 'What could I ask my friends to start a conversation?'), and finally, a theory of mind question (e.g. 'Who will be happy if I share my toys?'). The comprehension questions, much like the rest of the Social Narrative, should also be written from the first-person perspective, and should use positive and literal language. Do not, however, provide any picture clues.

The comprehension questions should be presented on their own page in a similar format to the questions illustrated in Figure 4.1. Circle time is a method used in the school system to promote self-esteem, to support the development of positive classroom relationships, and to develop a variety of skills such as communication, fine-motor, and assertiveness. The practice involves children sitting in a circle with their teacher and doing group activities, usually involving stories, group discussions, and songs with accompanying movements.

Questions

1. What does my class do at circle time?

2. What will I try to do during circle time songs?

3. Who will be happy?

FIGURE 4.1: Example of questions used at the end
of a Social Narrative to assess comprehension

Step 10: Reviewing the story

Well done! You have written your very own Social Narrative intervention! Before moving on to the next chapter, where we will look at how to physically present the story and implement it, it is time to reflect on what you have produced. Look over the story one last time to catch any errors. One important thing to watch for is the length and complexity of the story. Make sure that the story is not too long (which can cause lapsed attention) or too short (which can cause boredom and omit important information). The story should match the reading level of the child in both the language used and length. Use the checklist in Chapter 7 to see if the stories above and the ones you have created meet the requirements for a Social Narrative.

The next chapter outlines how to present and implement Social Narrative interventions. It also explains how long is needed before the intervention should be effective, solutions to common problems encountered, and how to maximize effectiveness.

5

Presenting and Implementing Social Narratives

How do I present the story?

Before pressing 'print', it is time to format your story so that it is presented in a way that optimizes learning. What follows are some guidelines on how to go about formatting Social Narratives.

1. Social Narratives should be presented as a booklet, just like a real book. Each page of the booklet should be A5 (5.8 x 8.3 inches) in size (that is, half of an A4 sheet, 8.3 x 11.7 inches).

2. The title of the story should be on the first page of the booklet, centred and **emboldened**. Nothing but the title should be on the first page.

3. The story you have written should be divided up onto separate pages in the booklet. Separate pieces of information should be chunked together. Information about the self could go on one page, for example, 'My name is Patrick. I go to Washington Special School.' Information about where to perform the targeted behaviour could go on the next page, for example, 'Every day at lunchtime we go to the playground. Children like to play together in the playground.'

4. Through chunking, the task of reading the story is made less complicated. When a task is too complicated, the ability of those on the autism spectrum to interpret and remember information can be reduced (Minshew and Williams 2008). This can also negatively impact the ability to correctly comprehend the sentences in a story (Desmarais *et al.* 2012). When information is presented on separate pages, this information can be examined for as long as necessary before turning the page. The individual is likely to be less distracted by the information that has gone before, or the information that comes after, allowing for deeper encoding.

5. Depending on the child's ability, sentences can either be presented together as a paragraph, or one sentence per line.

6. The text used should be black and sans serif, a font that does not have small protruding features at the end of strokes. These fonts are clearer to read. Some popular sans serif fonts are Arial, Tahoma and Futura. A good font for younger children is Comic Sans. The font size should be large enough for the child to read easily and comfortably. It is dependent on the amount of information per page, but 20pt in size is a good rule of thumb.

7. Pictures should be included to add visual support to the written text, except on the title page and comprehension question page.

8. On the last page of the booklet, the comprehension questions should be listed. A space underneath every question should be included for the child to write in an answer if needed.

9. Press the 'print' button.

10. Ideally, each page of the Social Narrative should be laminated. The story will be read every day with the child, and then used as a resource to refer to after the child has mastered the skill. Paper and card can easily rip with overuse. Accidents happen, and food and drink can be spilled on the booklet over time. If the pages are laminated, these spills can be easily cleaned. Furthermore, if the comprehension question page is laminated, children can write the answers to the comprehension questions in the spaces provided with a marker pen, which can be erased for the following day's session.

11. Time to bind the story together. There are two binding options. The first is to get a hole punch and punch three holes in the left hand margin of each page, equally spaced. The pages can then be tied together with string. Alternatively, if you have access to a spiral binder, you could use this to hold the pages together as a booklet.

How do I implement the story?

So now the story is written, formatted, printed and ready to use. Here is a list of easy-to-follow steps to implement your Social Narrative interventions.

1. Plan to read the story just before a time you would expect the target behaviour to occur. This means picking a time of the day the child is provided with an opportunity to display the targeted skill, for example, just before lunchtime at school or just before a trip to the playground. The story will therefore act like a prompt to perform the behaviour.

2. At this time every day, address the child by saying 'Time to read your story.' Reading the story every day maximizes the chances that the child will understand the lesson, and learning is strengthened.

3. Direct the child to an area that is quiet and free from distractions and other children.

4. Place the story directly in front of the child on an empty desk, kitchen table or work station. Any area where the child regularly does their homework or any occupational therapy exercises should be appropriate. Those with autism can become easily sidetracked in situations where there is sensory overload (Mesibov and Howley 2003). It is therefore imperative that Social Narratives be implemented in an environment that minimizes distractions for the child. Their attention should be focused on the story and not on distracting materials. At school, a clear work station is hard to find, so it is okay to leave work materials on the desk, for example, stationery and copy books.

5. Ensure the child is not engaging in any off-task or overtly disruptive behaviour. If the child is out of sorts, and is unlikely to be able to concentrate on the story for the duration, it is best to delay reading the story until the child has settled.

6. When reading the story, sit beside the child, but not in front of them. Again, we want the attention on the story itself and not on you. Figure 5.1 illustrates how you should sit.

FIGURE 5.1: Illustration of the appropriate way to position
the child and the adult while reading a Social Narrative

7. Ensure the child is looking at the Social Narrative. This
    is especially important when the child is unable to read
    the story independently. Even if the child appears to be
    listening intently, if they are not looking at the story, then
    they are missing out on the extra information they could
    obtain from the pictures.

8. The first time you read the Social Narrative, read it first to
    the child, then ask the child to read it back to you aloud.
    This means that the Social Narrative will be read twice
    on the first day. Thereafter, the child should read aloud
    the story once daily *to you*, unless unable to do so.

9. After the child has read their story, ask them the
    comprehension questions. Ask the child for a verbal or
    written answer, and determine if the responses provided
    are correct and appropriate based on the story. If the

questions are answered correctly, well done, you've finished the session! If the comprehension questions are answered incorrectly, ask all the comprehension questions again until there is 100 per cent accuracy in the responses. The answers should be explained to make sure the child truly understood the story. You may need to re-read the story with the child to make sure they understand.

10. After you have finished reading the story with the child, have it available for them to easily access during the rest of the day. You can also use its availability as a prompt to perform behaviour. For example, if the child's story is about not interrupting others when speaking in a group, the child could be encouraged to adopt the message of the story if it is within their line of sight when speaking with their peers.

11. Keep note of any behavioural changes so you can monitor any differences resulting from the intervention.

12. Read the story for around three weeks. Every child is different, however, and it is impossible to determine how long is needed for intervention success. Some children master the skill after their first reading; for others it can take weeks. Even if behaviour is observed after the first reading, don't stop reading the story immediately – fade the story from use gradually and monitor progress (refer to the fading procedure in the following Top Tip). If no changes are observed after three weeks, start questioning the suitability of the story. Refer to the 'Possible problems and solutions' section in this chapter for further information.

Top Tip: When we use fading, we attempt to remove the story from use, while maintaining the behavioural gains. There are a number of different fading procedures, the easiest being a reduction in the number of times a story is read. Instead of reading the story every day, reduce this to four times a week, to every second day, and so on. Alternatively, you could remove all factual sentences, leaving only the instructive sentences (or vice versa), and ask the comprehension questions. Or even just reduce the sessions to a question-and-answer session without reading the story.

Maximizing effectiveness

Use supporting interventions

There are a number of ways you can boost the effectiveness of your Social Narratives. One such way is to use a supporting intervention. The following lists easy-to-use interventions that may support the child to achieve their target behavioural goal.

1. A great way to help the child be more comfortable with the target behaviour is to practice it in a safe place with a familiar person. After the Social Narrative is read for the first time, the child may find it beneficial to role-play a social situation so that they can try out the behaviour in the story. The aim is to make them less anxious about trying it with their peers later.

2. A great idea for younger or non-verbal children is to use visual schedules to support Social Narrative interventions. Using a picture on their schedule for storytime right before the Social Narrative is read, and another picture of

playtime directly after the story is read, will help children make the connection between the story and playtime. A picture on their schedule of the targeted behaviour will also eliminate confusion as to what is expected.

3. Perhaps one of the simplest ways of supporting a Social Narrative intervention is to use aspects of applied behaviour analysis (ABA), such as prompting and reinforcement. The Social Narrative itself, read just before social behaviour is expected to be observed, acts as a prompt. A prompt can come in many forms including instructions, gestures, demonstrations and physical guidance. A prompt is really anything we can arrange or do to increase the likelihood of a correct response. In this way, Social Narratives are an instructional prompt. They instruct the child on how they should behave in social situations. We could use other prompts too, to increase their effectiveness. During the social situation, a verbal prompt like 'Remember your story' can be very effective. In the school classroom, posters in play areas highlighting the message of the Social Narrative, like 'Everyone is happy when we share toys', can also act as a prompt to perform certain behaviour.

4. Reinforcement is another ABA principle that can be used to support Social Narrative interventions. Reinforcement is anything we add or take away that increases a desired behaviour. Reinforcers that most children are familiar with include stickers for good behaviour or tokens that can be used to earn something desirable, for example, time on the computer or a new toy. You may find the activity book *Getting Along with Others* a useful tool in developing a reinforcement schedule. The details of this

book are listed in the Further Reading section at the end of this book.

5. What is important to remember when using reinforcement is that the reward should be immediate following the desired behaviour. In this way, the child will learn the relationship between the reward and the behaviour, making it more likely that the behaviour will be performed in the future.

6. Praise is another very effective form of reinforcement, depending on the child. A comment of 'Great job, you played with your friends great' can go a long way in motivating a child to perform the behaviour again in the future. Be specific if you use praise. Tell the child exactly what it was they have done correctly.

7. Of course, we would like the child to perform the behaviour without always having to prompt it or reinforce it. If you have decided to use either or both of these techniques, it is a good idea to fade them from use over time. The easiest fading procedure in this case is just to decrease the number of times you prompt and reinforce. For example, if you have been rewarding the child with stickers every time they say 'Hello', reduce this to one sticker for every two times they say 'Hello', or one sticker a day regardless of how many times they say 'Hello' in that day, and gradually fade the reward out altogether.

8. What we haven't considered so far is that the child's peers can also be barriers to successful social performance. Despite a child's best efforts, sometimes their peers remain unwilling to engage socially. For an effective social exchange to occur, all participants must be willing

and able to socialize. What follows is an example of a situation where the Social Narrative is effective, but social partners act as a barrier to success. It is inspired by true events.

John was being educated in a special school setting for children on the autism spectrum and other developmental disorders. He had a diagnosis of autistic disorder and a learning disability. He played well with the other children in his class. He regularly joined with another pupil to cooperatively build buildings and spaceships from Lego®. John found it difficult to talk to his friends, however. These play sessions were often in complete silence. When he did talk during play, it was passing remarks directed towards nobody in particular, which required no response, for example, 'This car is great.' John's Social Narrative focused on getting him to ask his play partners questions so that he could have a conversation. John loved his Social Narrative and looked forward to reading it every day. He took on board the message of the story after the first reading. At playtime on the first day of intervention, he asked his friend 'Do you like Transformers?', which was an interest of his, and a performance option in one of the instructive sentences in his story. His friend replied with a 'No', which finished the conversation. After subsequent readings, John started to create his own questions to ask on topics like television sitcoms and movies. His preferred play partner, however, would only respond with a 'Yes' or a 'No' when asked, while at other times he ignored the question. When John was paired with a more verbal child in the class for play, John's questions were well received and reciprocal conversation resulted.

9. This is an example of how a Social Narrative could be very effective at increasing social behaviour, but is hindered

because of factors external to the child. To avoid this situation, make sure the child has access to social partners who will provide the opportunities for them to practice their skill and positively reinforce their efforts. It may be necessary for the peer to receive a reciprocal intervention to encourage them to support the child's attempts at social behaviour. For example, a Social Narrative encouraging a child to join in play on the school playground where the peers actively exclude the child from their games will not be very effective. A school-wide initiative aimed at inclusion might be needed.

One story at a time

Another way of maximizing the effectiveness of a Social Narrative is to avoid overloading the child with information and instructions. Make sure you implement only one story at a time. Move on to a new story targeting a new behaviour only when the old story is finished and that behaviour is acquired.

Top Tip: When the child has mastered the skill in the story and it is no longer needed, make a Social Narrative library so the child can physically see their accomplishments, and access the stories if they ever need to.

Review once a day

To maximize the effectiveness of Social Narratives, the story should be read at the same time every day for the duration of the intervention. This establishes the story as part of the child's daily schedule, and appeals to the preference of those on the autism spectrum for routine (APA 2000).

Possible problems and solutions

A majority of children who receive Social Narratives love their stories and are attentive to them, which usually results in an increase in pro-social behaviour. The intervention is designed to be easy to write and to implement, appealing to both teachers and parents who often have issues with time constraints. From experience, very few problems are encountered using Social Narratives. There is always bound to be some hiccups, however. In the following section, I have listed solutions to problems that I have encountered in the past, along with issues that could conceivably arise when using Social Narratives.

1. PROBLEM: THE CHILD IS REFUSING TO READ THEIR STORY.

   SOLUTION: Every person is an individual with different strengths and weaknesses, and different likes and dislikes. It is impossible to create an intervention that suits all. Most children I have worked with enjoy reading their story. Those children who were averse to reading their story tended to be those with higher functioning autism or those diagnosed with Asperger's syndrome. There are a number of reasons why this could be the case. One common reason is that the story has factual errors. One particular child I worked with would moan whenever the story was produced. When asked what it was he disliked about the story, he said that it made him look like a baby. The story mentioned that he liked Thomas the Tank Engine, when in fact, his interest was in trains in general, and the mechanics of how they worked. Errors like this can insult the child's intelligence. Make sure that the story is edited before reading it with a child. If in doubt, ask the child for clarification.

Some children may react negatively to a story because it highlights an area of difficulty, a weakness of theirs, or a situation that provokes anxiety. In this instance, the child may become defensive and refuse to participate in the intervention plan. One way to tackle this issue is to include skills that the child has already mastered in the story. Use statements like 'I am really good at talking to my friends' and 'I am excellent at sharing my toys with my sister.' Statements like these can boost a child's self-esteem and reduce anxiety, making the rest of the story more acceptable.

Other children may not have a specific reason as to why they do not like reading the story. In this case, the best course of action is to get them more involved with the story development. Ask them to help you write or rewrite it. Talk about the target behaviour with them and their views on it. They may have a reason why they are not performing this behaviour. For example, you may be targeting a behaviour like initiating conversation with peers. The child, however, is reluctant to engage with the story you have created. When discussed with the child, it becomes apparent that they know how to initiate conversations, yet when they have tried to use this skill in the past, their efforts were not rewarded (e.g. the peer did not respond). This, quite understandably, makes them hesitant to try again.

The most important thing to remember is that it is never a good idea to force a child to read the story, or to use the story as a form of punishment for inappropriate behaviour. This could potentially discourage them from learning the targeted behaviour and going forward. Try to create a supportive learning environment, and make it a positive experience. Children should always enjoy reading their story.

2. PROBLEM: I HAVE BEEN READING THE STORY EVERY DAY AND FOLLOWING ALL THE GUIDELINES, BUT I SEE NO IMPROVEMENT.

SOLUTION: A bit of background knowledge helps to understand if change has taken place. One way to definitively check if there has been an improvement in the child's pro-social behaviour is to measure the targeted behaviour before, during and after intervention. Remember to recognize the progress of the individual rather than comparing their achievements to those of others. If the child displays a skill that they have never used before, this is a big achievement. They may not be performing that skill at the same level as their peers, but now they can now build on this newly acquired skill over time.

For some children it can take up to three weeks for a change in behaviour to be apparent. If over time you measure no change in behaviour, review the story, bearing a number of questions in mind. Is there anything that could be misunderstood/confusing/too literal? Is the story too complicated? Can the child read it easily and answer the comprehension questions with 100 per cent accuracy? Are there other skills the child needs to acquire first before they can master the targeted social behaviour? For example, are you targeting cooperative play when the child has yet to master parallel play? How many skills are you targeting in the story? Can the target skill be broken down further into smaller parts? For example, the story might be encouraging the child to play with their siblings. This skill could be broken down into steps for success, starting with a story about sitting beside their sibling in the playroom. When this is accomplished, another story could target sharing, and then a final story on playing a game together. Observe the situations you would expect the behaviour to be present in, for example, the playground. Are there peers available who are receptive to play? Are there ample opportunities for the child to display the skill?

If in doubt, ask somebody else, like a colleague or fellow parent, to review your story. Remember that there could also be reasons external to the story itself that could be hindering intervention success.

3. PROBLEM: THE CHILD CANNOT ANSWER THE COMPREHENSION QUESTIONS CORRECTLY.

SOLUTION: This is a simple one–the story is too complicated. Make the story shorter, simplify the language used, use shorter sentences, and try again. Remember that for the story to be successful, the child must not only be able to read it, but must also be able to comprehend it.

4. PROBLEM: THE CHILD LOVES THEIR STORY AND WANTS TO READ IT OVER AND OVER AGAIN, EVEN THOUGH THEY HAVE MASTERED THE SKILL.

SOLUTION: It's great that the child was so taken with Social Narratives. The story has been built into their routine. A common trait in ASD is to rely on routine to relieve stress and to lower anxiety. Implement a fading schedule for the Social Narrative and, if required, gradually introduce a new story.

5. PROBLEM: THE CHILD DOES NOT HAVE THE ATTENTION SPAN TO SIT AND READ THE STORY THROUGH FROM BEGINNING TO END.

SOLUTION: First, review the story to make sure it is as short and as simple as possible. To limit cognitive load, place flashcards with the main message of the story on the child's desk or above their bed at home. Alternatively, try presenting the story in a different format that may engage the child more and hold their attention. A Social Narrative could be presented as a PowerPoint presentation for those children who like working on computers. The story could also be adapted for a sing-along song for those children who respond well to music.

6. PROBLEM: IT HAS BEEN TWO WEEKS AND THE CHILD HAS MASTERED THE SKILL AND BECOME BORED WITH THE STORY.

SOLUTION: Start fading the story from use. The recommended period of three weeks can be a long time for some children. More advanced children may master the targeted behaviour after a couple of sessions. If this is the case, there is no need to persist with the story. If a child becomes bored and impatient, they may become disinclined to accept future Social Narratives. Additionally, if the child has mastered the skill and is performing the desired behaviour, they may become confused as to why you insist on continuing to read it with them. They may become anxious as a consequence. Fade the story from their routine and, if needed, substitute the story for a new one, targeting a different skill.

7. PROBLEM: I FIND IT HARD TO READ THE STORY AT THE SAME TIME EVERY DAY.

SOLUTION: Keeping to a tight schedule is better for the success of a Social Narrative. Those with ASD thrive on routine. The story is used as a prompt for behaviour, so it is best read just before the social situation. Of course this is not always practical, especially for teachers with large classes or busy parents. Try as best you can to be consistent. If you miss the designated time, don't abandon the idea of reading it that day – better late than never. If you know you are unlikely to be able to read it on a particular day, ask a friend, family member, colleague or another teacher to step in and take on the duty.

8. PROBLEM: I THOUGHT I HAD TIME TO READ THE STORY WITH THE CHILD EVERY DAY, BUT I AM JUST SO BUSY.

SOLUTION: The story and comprehension questions should only take a maximum of five minutes a day. They are designed to be undemanding on the adult's time. Nevertheless, home and school life can be hectic and unpredictable, so if you find that you are unable to continue, a solution may be to share the workload. Ask a special needs assistant for help or a fellow teacher or parent to take turns reading the story on alternate days. A story read by different people is better than no story at all.

The next chapter presents some results of research carried out supporting the use of Social Narratives with an autism population.

6

Research Supporting Social Narratives

Before deciding on an intervention, it is important to check that the intervention has been shown to work. If the child you are working with is on the autistic spectrum, it is particularly important to check that the intervention has worked with this population. As outlined throughout this book, children on the autism spectrum have unique learning characteristics that need to be taken into account before deciding on an intervention to try. What may work very well for children without a developmental disorder may not work at all for children with a developmental disorder.

The effectiveness of Social Narratives was experimentally investigated with 42 children on the autism spectrum between the ages of 4 and 18. These children were randomly divided into two separate groups. The first group, with 22 children assigned to it, received a tailor-made Social Narrative exactly like those described in this book. Each of the stories focused on a social skill the child was having difficulty with. These skills were decided based on questionnaire feedback and conversations with the child's teachers, special needs assistants and parents. After identifying social difficulties, the child was observed in a playtime situation to make sure that these skills were either completely absent, or occurred very rarely in comparison to their peers.

A research study investigating whether or not an intervention works needs to control for as many environmental influences as possible. For example, say a teacher decides to try a Social Narrative with a child in class. The teacher takes the child aside before playtime every day and reads the story with them for three weeks. The teacher sees a change in behaviour, and is amazed that the intervention works so well. How can we be sure, though, that it is the story that is having the effect and not something else? It could be that the increased one-to-one attention the child is receiving from the teacher is having an effect. Or it could even be that after the teacher has invested time to implement the intervention that they want to see change to make it worthwhile, and so sees behaviour change where none actually exists. What we need, then, is a way to control for as many environmental factors (like teacher attention) as possible, and an objective way of measuring if behaviour change has happened.

In this experiment, those administering the intervention were asked not to use any supporting interventions at the same time as the Social Narrative. This was to get a more accurate measure of the independent effect Social Narratives have on behaviour. Prompts to perform the behaviour (other than the Social Narrative itself) and reinforcement for good behaviour were also suspended during the intervention period.

The remaining 20 children received a control story. The control stories were also tailor-made for each child, taking into account their reading ability and interests, but these stories were unrelated to social skills. The control story was read in the same way as the Social Narrative, helping to control for any other factors that might influence the results.

Before the children read their story, videos were taken of them engaging with peers in free play. The stories were then read every day for three weeks, and videos were taken again after the three-week period had ended. The videos for each child were coded for the targeted behaviour, acting as an objective measure of behaviour change. The number of times the behaviour was present in the videos was counted both before and after the intervention. An average score for both the Social Narrative and control group was calculated before and after the intervention.

Figure 6.1 graphs the change in behaviour observed in the children from before they read their story intervention to after. As expected, the behaviour of the children who received the story unrelated to social skills (control group) remained relatively unchanged. There was the smallest of decreases in this group from before intervention to after, which can be accounted for by random fluctuation in their behaviours. We can assume, therefore, that the control stories had no effect on the social behaviour of children on the autism spectrum.

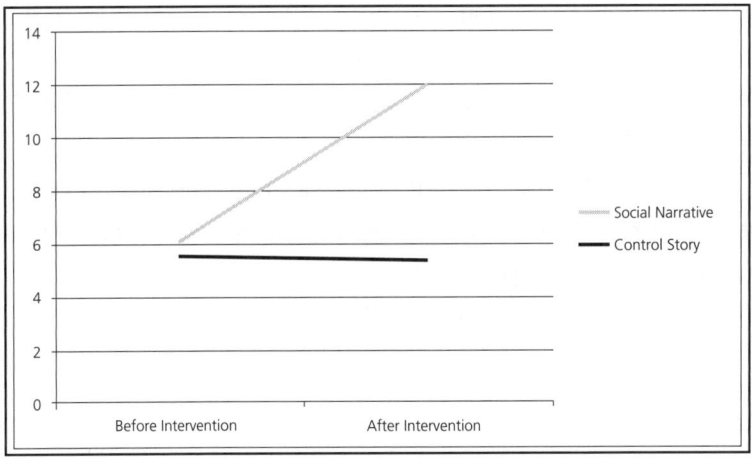

FIGURE 6.1: Mean target behaviour scores from before to after intervention for both the Social Narrative group and the control group

In contrast, the children who read the Social Narrative for the three-week period demonstrated a marked improvement in their targeted social skill. There was a large increase in the occurrence of the behaviours targeted by the Social Narratives from before intervention to after. It is unlikely that this large increase is due merely to random fluctuations in behaviour. We can also assume that it is the Social Narrative that is responsible for this change, as the control group was used as a comparison.

However, even if story interventions are found effective, teachers will not use them or implement them correctly, and participants will be non-compliant if they do not find them acceptable (Rapoff 2010). Furthermore, demonstrating that Social Narratives can change the behaviour of a child does not guarantee that the change is meaningful for the child or for those who implement the intervention. For example, say a Social Narrative encouraging a child to join in play is deemed effective using our video analysis above. There was an observed increase in the amount of time the child joined in play with their peers. Before the intervention, the child may have spent no time interacting with peers during playtime. After the intervention, there was evidence that the child did interact. However, the child might merely have run over to their peers in the class, sat with them for a second, and then returned to solitary play. Is this change meaningful?

To investigate if the child and the interventionist believed that the change observed following the Social Narrative was meaningful, the social validity of the intervention was measured. With its roots in ABA, social validity is the extent to which an intervention is viewed as acceptable and effective in a given context (Justice *et al.* 2011).

Social validity

Following intervention, children who received a Social Narrative intervention provided social validity feedback. Those who were capable were asked to read a number of statements and to answer 'Yes', 'No' or 'I Don't Know' to each. A total of

11 children from the Social Narrative group provided feedback. Table 6.1 provides a summary of their opinions.

Table 6.1: The questions and percentage of respondents to each response option, on the participant intervention evaluation form for Social Narratives

Statement	Yes	No	I Don't Know
I can make friends easier after reading my story	63.6	9.1	27.3
After reading my story I gained a new skill	54.5	45.5	0
I wanted to [target behaviour] after reading my story	72.7	9.1	18.2
Stories like my one are helpful for improving social skills	72.7	0	27.3
It is important to teach social skills	72.7	9.1	18.2
My story was difficult to use	18.2	72.7	9.1
My story was difficult to understand	9.1	81.8	9.1
My story helped me make friends	63.6	18.2	18.2

The majority of the children reported that they could make friends easier after reading their story (63.6%), and believed that their story had helped them make friends (63.6%). The majority of children also reported that they were motivated to perform the target behaviour after reading their story (72.7%). Very few thought their story was difficult to use (18.2%) or difficult to understand (9.1%). Thus, the children viewed Social Narratives quite favourably. They indicated that they liked their story, and felt the interventions were helpful, and easy to use and understand.

An interesting discrepancy in the findings is that some children (45.5%) reported that they had not gained a new skill after reading their story. This is despite observations of play situations showing behavioural change in targeted social behaviours following intervention. Bearing in mind that the intervention period lasted three weeks, it is possible that many children no longer considered the target behaviour a new skill by the time they were completing the social validity measure.

An additional measure of social validity was obtained through evaluation of the children's emotional reactions after reading their stories. Evaluations of whether a participant is happy with the intervention is one of the most important goals of social validation (Foster and Mash 1999). Each child was asked to record how they felt using a sheet of emoticons. The response options were happy, sad, mad, worried or confused. The child completed this each day after reading their story. Reports suggest that the majority of the children (78.2%) were happy after reading their story.

The children appeared to accept Social Narratives as an intervention. Some connected with their stories so much that they requested if they could bring the story they used at school home, and that more stories be made for them. One particular child found his story so useful that he told his teacher what social situations he found confusing and what topics he would like future stories to target. Children who were not part of the study also asked if they, too, could have their own story with their name in it. It seems as though children like the concept of owning their own story made just for them.

Teachers who implemented the Social Narratives also reported that the interventions were easy to implement in the classroom, easy to use, suitable for a wide variety of behaviours, and inexpensive. In fact, one mainstream school decided to use Social Narratives school-wide as a part of their social skills curriculum after one of their pupils participated in the study. They saw the benefits of using Social Narratives with all children, not just those on the autism spectrum. One teacher even took it a step further, suggesting Social Narratives could be adapted for adults, and wrote a script to increase her motivation to behave better in social situations.

The next chapter includes a checklist to help those writing Social Narratives, to make sure their stories conform to the development and implementation guidelines.

7

Checklist

Social Narratives are short stories aimed at developing the social skills of children. They have been developed with the learning characteristics of those on the autism spectrum in mind, but could be used with most children with social difficulties. It is hoped that the instructions to develop and implement Social Narratives have been clear. What follows is a quick reference guide. Use it to check if the story you have developed meets all the requirements of a Social Narrative. Once you become familiar with writing Social Narratives, this checklist also makes it possible to develop Social Narratives without having to re-read this whole book each time. An example of a completed Social Narrative is illustrated in Figure 7.1.

Deciding on the Rules for Snakes and Ladders

Megan's Story

My name is Megan.

I go to St Martin's primary school.

Usually my teacher is Ms Cleary.

After lunch every day we usually have game time in the classroom.

I usually like to play with the kitchen.

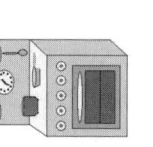

Sometimes we play group games.

I will try to join in the group games.

I will try to play nicely with the children in my class.

I usually play snakes and ladders with the children in my class.

Ms Cleary tries to change the people I play snakes and ladders with every day.

This is okay.

I will try to play snakes and ladders with the children Ms Cleary asks me to play with.

I will try to play nicely with the children I am asked to play with.

People can sometimes play games in different ways.

Sometimes people have different rules for snakes and ladders.

This is okay.

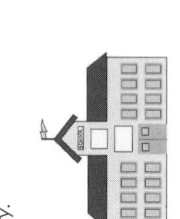

I will try to stay calm if people think that the rules of snakes and ladders are different to my rules.

I could take a deep breath to calm down.

I could ask my playmates what they think the rules of the game are.

I could ask them this before we start the game.

I could explain to them what I think the rules of snakes and ladders are.

We could decide together what rules we will use to play the game.

I will try to be calm if we choose to play by different rules.

I will try to play by the rules that we all agree on.

This is a good thing to do.

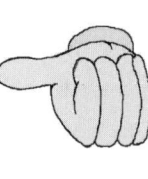

I will try to stay calm while playing games.

The children I play with will be happy if I play by the rules that we all agree on.

Questions

1. What does my class do at circle time?

2. What will I try to do during circle time songs?

3. Who will be happy?

FIGURE 7.1: Example of a Social Narrative

Writing checklist

1. Identify a target behaviour that the child has the ability to master.

2. Focus on positive behaviours, for example, using a quiet voice rather than discouraging shouting.

3. Match the length of the Social Narrative to the reading ability of the child.

4. Did you incorporate the child's interests into the story?

5. State where the behaviour is expected to occur, for example, playground, playtime etc.

6. Explain the who, what, where and when of a situation using factual sentences. Explain the how of a situation using instructive sentences. Make sure that there is an even balance of factual and instructive sentences in your story.

7. Avoid definitive instructions like 'I will', and use phrases like 'I will try to' or 'I could' instead.

8. Use the first-person perspective.

9. Watch the language used. Make sure it is literal and positive.

10. Include pictures to reinforce the story.

11. Make sure your title also follows all the guidelines for writing a Social Narrative.

12. Write some comprehension questions.

The final chapter of this book provides a number of sample stories that target a variety of social skills.

8

Sample Stories

Social Narratives can be used to target an infinite number of social skills. The only limit is your imagination. This chapter includes some sample stories on common social topics. The sample Social Narratives included in this book are inspired by stories used successfully with children on the autism spectrum, and target difficulties commonly experienced by this population, although the children, schools, teachers and parents named in these stories are fictitious. Any resemblance to actual persons, living or dead, or actual events, is purely coincidental.

These stories are intended as a guide to writing Social Narratives. If you wish to use one of the stories in this chapter, remember to personalize the story for the child who is to receive it. Remember to include the interests of the child, rather than the interests included in these stories. Change details that are incorrect, such as the child's name or school. Additionally, the stories that follow are written for children with a variety of target behaviours. The children who received them were functioning at different levels. Please ensure that the stories that you use are tailored to your child's reading competencies. These stories were written for either a home or a school setting. Feel free to adapt them for any other setting as required.

You may notice that the sample stories that are presented in this chapter do not follow the presentation guidelines outlined in Chapter 5. They are not laminated and bound, do not include pictures or comprehension sessions, and the information is not chunked onto separate pages. However, suggestions are provided on where to break up the information onto separate pages, and are indicated by a continuous black line.

Each of the stories has some background information on the child they were used with or the behaviour targeted. You may see some similarities between these children and the ones you are working with in terms of social skills deficits and interests. It is hoped that these stories will clearly demonstrate how a Social Narrative is written, and will inspire you when creating your own.

Greetings

Waving to say hello

BACKGROUND: The first two sample stories (this one and the one that follows) focus on one of the most basic of social skills, greetings. Social Narratives focusing on greetings are great stories for those children with very limited social skills. This Social Narrative was written for Olivia. Olivia was a very bright, energetic, non-verbal child. This story focused on waving to other people to say hello. It was used in conjunction with prompts. After reading the story, Olivia's mum would manipulate Olivia's hand to show her how to wave. When out walking, Olivia's mum would also use verbal prompts to encourage Olivia to wave to say hello.

Child's interests: Teddy Woo Woo (her teddy bear).

Title: Waving to say hello – Olivia's story

My name is Olivia.
I live with my mum and dad.

Sometimes I go for a walk with mum.
I usually bring my Teddy Woo Woo.

Sometimes on our walk people wave at me to say hello.
I will try to wave too.

I will try to wave to say hello.
I will try to look at who is waving at me.

I will try to lift my hand into the air.
I will try to move my hand from side to side.
This is called a wave.

I will try to wave to say hello.
When people wave at me I will try to wave too.

I will try to wave to say hello.
People will be happy if I wave to say hello.
This is a good thing to do.

Saying hello

BACKGROUND: This Social Narrative was written for Abdullah, who had some verbal abilities. Much like Olivia in the previous sample story, Abdullah displayed limited social skills. Abdullah was being educated in a special needs unit attached to a mainstream integrated school. He had two classmates. Abdullah and his classmates would spend time during the day with the other children in the school to encourage the development of social skills. This story focused on how to say hello to others.

Child's interests: Thomas the Tank Engine and playing chasing in the yard.

Title: Saying hello – Abdullah's story

My name is Abdullah.

I go to Lincoln kindergarten.

Usually my teacher is Ms Mullins.

I will try to say hello to Ms Mullins and my other teachers.

I will try to say hello when I see them in the morning.

Sometimes I play with Thomas the Tank engine in the classroom in the morning.

Sometimes the other children in my class play with something else.

I will try to say hello to the children in my class.

I will try to say hello to the children in my class when I see them in the morning.

There are other children in my school.
I will try to say hello to the other children in my school.

Sometimes I play chasing in the yard with my friends.
I will try to say hello to my friends when I am playing with them.

I will try to say hello to my friends when I see them.
My teacher and my friends will be happy if I say hello to them.

Developing social etiquette

Standing too close when talking

BACKGROUND: This is David's story, which is about allowing for personal space when talking to members of a family. When David was talking with a member of his family, he would often stand very close to them. With his siblings, this often resulted in David being right in their face when they were having a conversation. David has really developed his interpersonal communication skills. It was important that his Social Narrative did not discourage him from continuing to communicate freely with his family. It was also important that David did not become anxious when talking to others. This sample story provides an example of how positive statements such as 'I am great at talking to my brother and sister' can be incorporated into a Social Narrative to protect a child's self-esteem.

Child's interests: Ninjas and airplanes.

Title: Standing an arm apart when I talk – David's story

My name is David.
I live with my mum, my dad, my sister Clara and my little brother Chris.
We all live together in our house in Newcastle.

I am great at talking to my brother and sister.
I am great at talking to my mum and dad.
Sometimes I talk about Ninjas or airplanes.

I will try to stand an arm apart when I talk to my family.

People like having some space between them when they talk.

I will try and keep some space between me and the person I am talking to.

I will try and keep some space between me and Clara when we talk.

I will try and keep some space between me and Chris when we talk.

I will try and keep some space between me and my mum when we talk.

I will try and keep some space between me and my dad when we talk.

I will try and keep some space between me and anyone else I talk to.

Keeping some space means that when I stand with one arm straight out I cannot touch the person I am speaking to.

I will try to keep some space between me and the person I am talking to.

I will try to stand an arm's length away from who I am talking to.

I will try and keep this amount of space between us when we are talking.

This is a good thing to do.

My family will be happy if I keep some space between me and the person I am talking to.

Politely getting attention

BACKGROUND: Margaret liked sharing her love of internet videos with her parents. She would carry her phone with her at all times, and would be constantly looking at her favourite clips and new discoveries. When she found something particularly amusing, she showed it to others. Margaret would be so eager for her parents to watch the video clip that she would interrupt them regardless of the situation. This included when they were in the middle of a conversation, on the phone, paying at checkouts at the shop, or while they were doing important tasks. Margaret would get frustrated if her parents did not pay her attention immediately. This story focused on helping Margaret develop a plan of action for getting attention in a socially acceptable manner.

Child's interests: Videos on the internet, particularly 'ultimate fail' videos, which she finds very amusing.

Title: Getting my parent's attention – Margaret's story

My name is Margaret.
I live with my mum and dad.

Sometimes I want to tell mum and dad something.
Sometimes I want to tell them about a funny video on YouTube.

Sometimes I want to show mum and dad something.
Sometimes I want to show them the funny video on YouTube.

I will try to get mum and dad's attention politely.

I will try and look at mum or dad when I want their attention.

I will try to ask them to watch or listen to me.

I will try to ask them only once.

I will try to wait until they are ready to pay me attention.

I will try to thank mum and dad for paying me attention.

This is a good thing to do.

I will try to get mum and dad's attention politely.

Mum and dad will be happy if I get their attention politely.

Paying a compliment

BACKGROUND: This story was developed for Santiago to encourage him to think of the feelings of others. It was hoped that this would improve his social relationship with his sisters. His sisters were very caring and would regularly do things for Santiago, including indulging his interests and playing the games that Santiago wanted to play.

Child's interests: Playing Mario Kart on his Nintendo® Wii and painting pictures.

Title: Saying nice things to people – Santiago's story

My name is Santiago.
I live with my mum, dad, Carolina and Jessica.

I will try and say nice things to my sisters.
Saying nice things to my sisters makes them feel good.

I could say to Carolina 'I like the sweater you picked to wear today.'
I could say to Jessica 'You are so kind to share your toys with me.'
I could say to Carolina 'You are a great sister.'
I could say to Jessica 'You are a great sister.'
I could say a different nice thing to my sisters.

Sometimes I play games with Carolina and Jessica.
Sometimes we play Mario Kart on the Wii.

Sometimes we paint pictures.
Sometimes we play something else.
It is a good time to say something nice to my sisters when we are playing.

I will try to say nice things when I am playing.
I will try to say nice things to my sisters when we play together.
I could say to Carolina 'You did great in that Mario Kart race.'
I could say to Jessica 'I really like the picture you drew.'
I could say a different nice thing to my sisters.

Saying nice things to my sisters makes them feel good.
This is a good thing to do.

My sisters will be happy if I say nice things to them.

Good sportsmanship

BACKGROUND: This story was developed for Nicola to motivate her to be a better 'sport' when playing games with others. She tended to be both a poor winner and a poor loser. If she won, she would usually gloat. If she lost, she would be visibly upset and often verbally abuse the winner of the game. This would even be the case if her teacher was playing a game with her. If Nicola recognized that she was about to lose, she would often prevent people from moving their piece, or move her piece forward instead. As a direct consequence of this behaviour, the children in her class did not like to play with her. Nicola was quite academically advanced, with above-average ability. This story targets the behaviour of sportsmanship under the title of 'Playing nicely with my friends'. For less able children with similar issues, it would be better to break this story into three separate skills: cheating, being a good winner, and being a good loser. Each of these skills could be the focus of a different story and presented sequentially so that sportsmanship is built up over time.

Child's interests: Playing on the jungle gym and playing board games.

Title: Playing nicely with my friends – Nicola's story

My name is Nicola.

I go to St Mary's National School.

Usually my teacher is Mr Lee.

There is usually playtime at school.
Sometimes I play in the yard on the jungle gym.
Sometimes I play in the classroom. Sometimes I even play board games.
I will try to play nicely.

There is usually someone with me when I play during the day.
Sometimes a teacher is with me and sometimes my friends are with me.
I will try to play nicely with my teacher.
I will try to play nicely with my friends.

I will try to follow the rules of the game when I am playing.

Sometimes when I play games I am winning.
I will try to remember to play nicely and be a good winner.
I will try to play nicely.

I will try to make my friends feel good when they are losing.
I could say something like 'Do not worry, I am sure you will catch up.'
I could say 'well done' after my friends take a go.
My friends like it when I make them feel good about losing.

Sometimes when I play games I am the one who is losing.
This is okay.
I will try to play nicely and be a good loser.

I will try to let my friends take their go of the game even if it means they will win.

This is a good thing to do.

I could say 'well done' to my friends if they are winning.

I will try to be a good winner when I am playing games.

I will try to be a good loser when I am playing games.

My friends will be happy if I play nicely.

Developing social communication

Joining in a conversation

BACKGROUND: This story was developed for Josh to improve his social communication skills. Josh went to school in an integrated setting. At lunch and playtime, he would often sit by himself and read a book or look at an atlas. Other children in the class would often try to start conversations with him, but Josh would be unresponsive. He would sit in a group with his classmates, like at game time, but ignore the conversations going on around him. This aim of this Social Narrative was to motivate Josh to join in conversations with his classmates.

Child's interests: Atlases, reading, Nintendo® DS, cartoons and collecting cards and figurines.

Title: Joining in my friends' conversations – Josh's story

My name is Josh.

I go to Castleview primary school.

Usually my teacher is Ms Corcoran.

There are a lot of activities at school.

Usually I have schoolwork to do.

Sometimes I have a history lesson.

Sometimes I have a quiz.

Sometimes there is free time at school when I can relax and do what I want to do.

Sometimes I look at an atlas.

Sometimes I read a book.

Sometimes I sit with my friends in my class and we might play a game.

I will try to have conversations with my friends during free time.

My friends like it when I have conversations with them when I am sitting or playing a game with them.

I will try to listen to what my friends say.

I will try to answer my friends when they ask me a question.

I will try to join in my friends' conversations.

I could ask my friends questions when we are having a conversation.

I could say 'Do you like this game?'

I could say 'Do you have a DS?'

I could say 'What is your favourite cartoon?'

I could say 'Do you collect anything like cards or figurines?'

I could ask them something else.

It is a good idea to have conversations with people when I am sitting with them or playing a game with them.

I will try to answer my friends when they talk to me during free time.

I will try to ask my friends questions.

I will try to listen to what they say.

My friends will be happy if I have conversations with them.

Starting a conversation

BACKGROUND: This Social Narrative was written to motivate Thomas to start conversations with his classmates. Thomas was good at parallel play. He would quite happily choose a game during choice time and sit with his classmates in a circle. During playtime, however, he would be very quiet, and never initiated any conversations.

Child's interests: Reading books and cooking.

Title: Talking to my friends – Thomas' story

My name is Thomas.
I go to Leinster school.
Usually my teacher is Mary.

Sometimes there is free time at school when I play with my friends.
Sometimes I have choice time in the classroom.
Sometimes I sit at a table with my friends during choice time.

I will try to talk to my friends during choice time.
I could say 'hello'.

My friends like it when I talk to them.

I could say 'What did you pick for choice time?'

I could say 'Do you like books?'

I could say 'Do you like cooking?'

I could say something else.
This is a good thing to do.

I will try to talk to my friends during choice time.
I will try to ask my friends questions when we are playing.

My friends will be happy if I talk to them.

Starting a conversation

BACKGROUND: The target behaviour in this story is the same as the last, starting a conversation. This Social Narrative, written for Anthony, is more advanced. Two stories on the same topic have been included to illustrate how Social Narratives are written for different ability levels. Anthony's story is written using paragraphs, whereas the previous story had one sentence per line. Much like Thomas in the last story, Anthony had difficulty initiating conversation. This story was written to explain to Anthony how to go about starting conversations.

Child's interests: WWE wrestling, computer games and playing on the PlayStation.

Title: Starting conversations with my classmates – Anthony's story

My name is Anthony. I go to Clooney National School. Usually my teacher is Mr Rydal.
There are other people in my class too. The people in my class are called my classmates.

Sometimes there is free time at school when I don't have to do work. I can talk to the people in my class at this time. I have free time at lunch or on the yard. Sometimes I have extra free time when I am allowed to play games with my classmates.
I will try to talk to my classmates during free time.

When I am talking with my classmates we are having a conversation.
I will try to have conversations with my classmates.

Someone always has to start a conversation. Someone has to bring up a topic to talk about. Sometimes my classmates will not start a conversation with me.

This is okay. I will try to start a conversation with my classmates.

I could start a conversation with my classmates by telling them about what I like.

I could talk to them about wrestling.

I could talk about my favourite video game.

I could start a conversation with my classmates by asking them a question.

When I am playing with my classmates it is a good time to ask them questions about themselves. I will try to ask my classmates questions about themselves when we are talking or playing together.

I could say 'Do you own a PlayStation?'

I could say 'What are you favourite video games?'

I could say 'What do you think of this board game?'

I could ask them something else.

Talking to my classmates and asking them questions is a good thing to do. I will try to start conversations with my classmates during free time. I will try to start conversations by telling my classmates about something that I like. I will try to start conversations by asking my classmates questions about themselves. My classmates will be happy if I start conversations with them during free time.

Listening to others

BACKGROUND: Many individuals on the autism spectrum often avoid looking at the face, or in the eyes, of their conversation partner. This Social Narrative was used successfully with Damien to improve the amount of time he spent looking at the face of children talking to him and children he was talking to.

Child's interests: Reading and swimming.

Title: Looking at my friends' faces – Damien's story

My name is Damien.

I go to Morningside School.

Usually my teacher is Ms Keegan.

There are usually lots of fun things to do at school.

Sometimes I read.

Sometimes I go swimming.

Sometimes I play games with my friends in the yard or in the classroom.

Usually people talk to each other when they are playing games or eating lunch together at school.

Sometimes when I am playing with my friends we talk to each other.

Usually people look at each other's faces when they talk to each other.

I will try to look at my friends' faces when we talk to each other.

When people are talking they like to know that they are being listened to.

I will try to show my friends that I am listening to them.

I can do this by looking at their faces.

I will try to look at my friends' faces when we talk to each other.

My friends are happy when I show them I am listening by looking at their faces when they are talking to me.

I will try to show my friends that I am listening.

I will try to look at my friends' faces when they are talking.

Sometimes when I am with my friends I am the one who is talking.

I will try to show my friends that I am talking to them and not to someone else.

I can do this by looking at their faces.

I will try to look at my friends' faces when I am talking to them.

This is a good thing to do.

I will try to look at my friends' faces when we talk to each other.

I will try to move my eyes so I am looking at their face.

I will try to look at my friends' faces when they are talking to me.

I will try to look at my friends' faces when I am talking to them.

Making friends

Making friends at the park

BACKGROUND: This story was written for Mohammad. Mohammad usually went to the park after school with his mum and brother. His mum had tried to get Mohammad more involved in the group games that were organized at the park. Mohammad preferred to play by himself in the playground, spending most of his time on the swings. He would show an interest in the games being played, but would not join in. This story was written to encourage Mohammad to make friends in the park, by initiating play and joining in organized games.

Child's interests: Superheroes, especially Spiderman.

Title: Making friends in the playground
– Mohammad's story

My name is Mohammad.
I live in Perth with my mum, my dad, and my brother Ibrahim.

After school mum usually takes me and Ibrahim to the park.
I usually play on the swings in the playground.

There are usually other children in the playground.
I will try to make friends with the children in the playground.

I could ask the children at the playground if they would like to play a game.
We could play chasing.

We could play superheroes.

I could pretend to be Spiderman.

I could play something else with the children in the playground.

Sometimes the children in the playground are already playing a game.

I could ask them if I could join in their game.

Sometimes the children are playing a big game of hide and go seek.

I could play hide and go seek too.

I will try to make friends with the children in the playground.

This is a good thing to do.

Mum will be happy if I try to play with the children in the playground.

New friends in a group

BACKGROUND: This Social Narrative was written for Liam. Liam had the same two friends from his class at school for two years. A new boy joined Liam's class this year. Liam's friends have shown an interest in the new boy, and have invited him to play with them. Liam disliked this change, and became very anxious and worried. He told his parents that he thought the new boy was trying to 'steal' his friends. This story was written to lower Liam's anxiety and to encourage Liam to incorporate the new boy into his social circle.

Child's interests: Match Attack cards.

Title: Making new friends – Liam's story

My name is Liam.

I go to St Mary's National School.

Usually I play with Martin and John at school.

In September a new boy called Christopher joined our class.

Martin and John like playing with Christopher.

This is okay.

Martin and John like playing with me too.

I will try to make friends with Christopher.

I can make friends with Christopher by playing games with him.

I will try to play games with Christopher.

I will try to let him join in with me, Martin and John.

I could ask Christopher if he wants to play Match Attack cards with us.

We could play chasing together in the yard.

We could play something else.

I could be Christopher's friend by letting him sit with us during lunchtime.

I could let Christopher talk with us during playtime.

This is a good thing to do. Martin and John will be happy if I make friends with Christopher.

Playing with others

Playing with siblings

BACKGROUND: This story was developed for Jason, who lived at home with his dad and typically developing older brother. Jason's dad and brother would have playtime every night, which Jason never joined, despite verbal encouragement. He preferred to play separately with his Thomas the Tank Engine toy. This Social Narrative attempted to motivate Jason to join in play with his family.

Child's interests: Thomas the Tank Engine.

Title: Joining in play – Jason's story

My name is Jason.
I live with my dad and brother John.

Sometimes John and Dad play together in the playroom.

I will try to join in play with John and Dad.

I could pass them the ball.

I could sit with John and Dad.

I could play with Thomas the Tank Engine with John and Dad.

I will try to play with John and Dad.

John and Dad will be happy if I play with them.

Participating in group activities

BACKGROUND: This particular story was developed for Daniel. Every day at Daniel's school there was circle time. The children in his class would sit in a circle, the teacher would play the guitar, and the children, special needs assistants and teacher would sing and do actions to various songs. Daniel, who loved music, really enjoyed circle time. He could not join in with the songs' actions because of his issues with manual dexterity. He did, however, have the ability to clap. His special needs assistant would model the clapping behaviour for him during circle time, but he was never observed joining in and clapping. This story explains how to clap during circle time.

Child's interests: Humming along to music.

Title: Joining in circle time – Daniel's story

My name is Daniel.
I go to St Augustin's Special School.

There are lots of things to do at school.
Sometimes we have circle time when we sing songs and read books.

I will try to join in circle time.

Some songs need us to clap our hands.
I will try to clap my hands during circle time songs.

I will try to put my two hands together to make a clapping noise.

My teacher will be happy if I try to clap along.

When I hear the music I will try to put my two hands together and start clapping.

I will try to clap along to circle time songs.

Choosing a game

BACKGROUND: This Social Narrative was written for Dylan. Dylan had great game-playing skills, and would play well with his brother Eric at home. Dylan loved Harry Potter. He had received a Harry Potter Monopoly set for Christmas one year. Since then, he has insisted on only playing this game and no other. Eric has become tired of the Monopoly game and is becoming disinclined to play with Dylan as a consequence. This story teaches Dylan that he can still play his favourite game, but in moderation. It teaches him to take turns with his brother when choosing what game to play.

Child's interests: Harry Potter.

Title: Choosing a game – Dylan's story

My name is Dylan.

I live with Mum, Dad and Eric.

Sometimes I play with my Harry Potter toys in my bedroom.

Sometimes I play board games with Eric in the kitchen.

I sometimes choose to play Harry Potter Monopoly.

This is okay.

Sometimes Eric wants to play a different game.

This is okay too.

I will try to take turns with Eric to choose a game to play.

I could choose a game to play first.
I could pick Harry Potter Monopoly.
I could pick the Harry Potter snap cards.
I could pick something else.

I could then try to let Eric choose a game.
I will try to stay calm if Eric picks a game I don't like.
I will try to let Eric have his turn.

I could let Eric choose a game to play first.
Then I could choose a game.

Taking turns choosing a game is a good thing to do.
Eric and Mum will be happy if I take turns choosing games.

Sharing

BACKGROUND: This Social Narrative focuses on sharing behaviour. Sharing is an important step in developing cooperative game-playing skills. Before a child can interact with other children in cooperative play, they must first learn to tolerate other people touching the same toys as them. This story was written for Michael, who had trouble sharing. His favourite toy in the classroom was the toy garage. He disliked other children touching it at all, or putting their cars anywhere close to it. When the teacher organized games in the classroom, Michael would keep the board, counters and dice to himself, and play alone.

Child's interests: Playing on the computer and toy cars.

Title: Sharing when I play – Michael's story

My name is Michael.
I go to Beaufort National School.
Usually my teacher is Ms Curtis.

There are lots of things to do at school.
Sometimes I play games on the computer.
Sometimes I play with cars or board games with my friends.
Sometimes I play with other toys with my friends.

I will try to share when I am playing with my friends.
I could share the toy cars.
I could let my friends put their cars in the car garage.
I could let my friends drive their cars on the road.

I could share the counters to play the board game.
I could share the dice.

I could share my computer games.

I will try to share whatever toys I am playing with.

I will try to let my friends have a turn when we are playing games.
Sharing is a good thing to do.

My friends will be happy when I share and let them have a turn.

Joining in cooperative play

BACKGROUND: This Social Narrative was written for Chris with the aim of developing his cooperative play. Chris had one-to-one tuition at a special needs school. During the school day, children from a different class would come to have playtime in Chris' classroom, so he could have social interaction. Chris has made significant improvements in his social skills since starting school. He is great at parallel play, often moving his toys to where the other children are sitting, and showing an interest in what they are doing. This Social Narrative was written to encourage him to take the next step and to engage in more cooperative play, for example, sharing play materials for a common goal.

Child's interests: Play dough, playing in the sandpit and playing with the toy garage.

Title: Playing with my friends – Chris' story

My name is Chris.

I go to Thornton pre-school.

Usually my teacher is Sarah.

Sometimes children from a different class come into my classroom.

Sometimes other boys and girls want to play with me and the toys in my classroom.

This is okay.

I will try to play with my friends.

I could give my friends some play dough.

I could build a sand castle with my friends in the sandpit.

I could make a jigsaw with my friends.

I could race cars with my friends using the garage.

I could share something else with my friends.
I will try to play with my friends.

It is good to play with my friends.
My friends will be happy if I play with them.

Joining in cooperative play

BACKGROUND: This story, written for Patrick, also targets cooperative play, but in a more advanced way. It recognizes the importance of conversation in cooperative play, of joining in rule-based play, and in cooperative pretend play.

Child's interests: Super Mario, action figures and building with blocks.

Title: How do I play with my friends? – Patrick's story

My name is Patrick. I go to Matheson Primary School.
Usually my teacher is Ms Pertl.

There are lots of boys and girls in my class.
They are my friends.

Sometimes Ms Pertl lets the class play with toys in the classroom.
Sometimes I play with action figures.
Sometimes I build something with blocks.

I will try to play with my friends.

I could sit beside my friends and play with what they are playing with.
When I am sitting with my friends I will try to talk to them.
I could ask them questions about the game they are playing.

I could say 'Can I play too?'

I could say 'How do you play this game?'

I could ask my friends something else.

I could ask my friends if they would like to play with what I am playing with.

I could ask them if they want to play with my action figures.

I could ask them if they would like to pretend to be Super Mario with me.

I could ask them if they would like to play something else.

This is a good thing to do.

My friends will be happy if I play with them.

My friends will be happy if I talk to them when we are playing.

Developing rule-orientated game-playing skills
Deciding on the rules of a game

BACKGROUND: This story was developed for Megan. Megan was being educated in an integrated setting and had good communication skills. She had a number of social difficulties that prevented her from developing and maintaining friendships. Her teacher had developed a number of initiatives to help Megan integrate better. During free time, Megan was prone to playing alone with her favourite toy, the kitchen. To encourage Megan to mix with the children in the class, Megan's teacher introduced board game time. Each day, Megan would play a board game of her choosing (always snakes and ladders) with different classmates. Megan reacted badly when the rules of the game were not followed, however. Her classmates were not cheating, but had different interpretations of the rules. For example, some children each roll the dice and decide who goes first by whoever rolls the highest number, or some children insist a player needs to roll the exact number of squares remaining on their last go to win the game. Megan would often get into verbal arguments and appear quite stressed if her rules were not followed. She would insist that she be allowed to pick her playmates based on the rules they adhered to. This story was developed to help Megan calm down during game play, to prepare her for the possibility of different rules, and to provide her with a strategy of clarifying the rules in a socially appropriate way.

Child's interests: Playing with the kitchen in the classroom, and snakes and ladders, the board game.

Title: Deciding on the rules for snakes
and ladders – Megan's story

My name is Megan.

I go to St Martin's primary school.

Usually my teacher is Ms Cleary.

After lunch every day we usually have game time in the classroom.

I usually like to play with the kitchen.

Sometimes we play group games.

I will try to join in the group games.

I will try to play nicely with the children in my class.

I usually play snakes and ladders with the children in my class.

Ms Cleary tries to change the people I play snakes and ladders with every day.

This is okay.

I will try to play snakes and ladders with the children Ms Cleary asks me to play with.

I will try to play nicely with the children I am asked to play with.

People can sometimes play games in different ways.

Sometimes people have different rules for snakes and ladders.

This is okay.

I will try to stay calm if people think that the rules of snakes and ladders are different to my rules.

I could take a deep breath to calm down.

I could ask my playmates what they think the rules of the game are.

I could ask them this before we start the game.

I could explain to them what I think the rules of snakes and ladders are.

We could decide together what rules we will use to play the game.

I will try to be calm if we choose to play by different rules.

I will try to play by the rules that we all agree on.

This is a good thing to do.

I will try to stay calm while playing games.

The children I play with will be happy if I play by the rules that we all agree on.

Coping with cheating playmates

BACKGROUND: This story was developed for Noah who had a preoccupation with cheating when playing games. Much like the previous sample story, this story also focuses on trying to get the child to relax and calm down during game time. In this instance, however, Noah was correct with regards other children cheating in the game. For example, some of the children in his class had a tendency to pretend their hand slipped so they could roll the dice again. Noah would get very upset when this happened, and would often shout and cry. The teacher suspected that some children might have been trying to get this emotional reaction intentionally. This is a good example of a story that is used in conjunction with another intervention. While Noah received this story on how to cope with cheating in a socially acceptable way, the teacher also focused on the other children in the class using a different intervention to promote fair play.

Child's interests: Loves doing projects. He likes to use the computer and books to look up facts about any topic. He then presents all this information in a folder.

Title: Relaxing when I am playing
with my friends – Noah's story

My name is Noah.
I go to Mount Carmichael Boy's School.
Usually my teacher is Ms Byrne.

I do a lot during the school day.
Sometimes I do projects and have to find out facts to put them together.

Sometimes I play with my classmates in the yard.
Sometimes Ms Byrne lets me play games with my classmates.
Sometimes we play with the blocks.
Sometimes we play board games.

I will try to relax when I am playing with my friends.
I could say 'well done' after they take a go of a board game.

I could let my friends decide on the rules of a game.
I will try to relax if my classmates make up rules I have never heard before.

Sometimes when I am playing games with my classmates they do things that I may not like.
Sometimes I might think that my classmates are cheating.
I will try and relax.

I will try and explain the rules of the game.
I will try to listen to what my classmates have to say.
I will try and stay calm.

My classmates might make mistakes.
Sometimes their hand might slip when they are rolling a dice.
They might want to take their go again.
This is okay.

I will try to relax.

I will try to let them take their turn again.

I could say to them 'You can take your go again but be careful next time.'

People play games to have fun.

Sometimes they do not care about the rules.

I will try to stay happy even if things go wrong.

I will try to stay calm.

I will try to think of games as just a bit of fun.

This is a good thing to do.

My friends will be happy if I relax when I am playing games with them.

Playing by the rules of the game

BACKGROUND: This story was developed for William, who had a tendency to cheat when playing games. He loved to play board games, and loved winning. It is important to note that besides his cheating behaviour, William displayed some sportsmanlike qualities. He would congratulate others on winning, and was a gracious winner. His usual cheating tactics would be to roll the dice and say his hand slipped if he rolled an unfavourable number. If he knew he was about to win, he would also get very impatient with his playmates. He would tell them to hurry up, and skip them so he could have a turn quicker. The aim of this story was to encourage William to play fairly and by the rules.

Child's interests: Lego®, Lego and more Lego.

Title: Playing fairly with my friends – William's story

My name is William.

I go to Monrose National School.

Usually my teacher is Mr Phillips.

Sometimes at school I play games with my friends in my class.

Sometimes we play with Lego and build spaceships.

Sometimes we play board games together.

I will try to play fairly with my friends.

Playing fairly means to follow the rules of the game.

I will try to follow the rules of the game.
This is a good thing to do.

I will try to let everyone take their turn.
I will try to roll the dice when it is my turn.
I will try to roll the dice once.
I will try to move my counter the number of spaces that are shown on the dice.
I will try to then pass the dice to the next person in the circle.
I will try to let everyone in the circle take their turn.

Sometimes people take a long time to take their go.
This is okay.
It will be my turn again soon.

I will try to stay in my place in the circle.
I will try to keep my counter in the correct spot when I am waiting.
I will try to wait for my turn.

I will try to play fairly with my friends.
My friends will be happy if I play fairly with them.

Focusing on the child's interests

Getting involved in other people's interests

BACKGROUND: Peter was a very able, articulate child who had a special interest in chess. He would often talk at length about different chess strategies to anybody who would listen. His classmates did not share his love of chess, however, and had become disinterested in talking to Peter as a consequence. This Social Narrative was written to motivate Peter to expand his topics of conversation to include the interests of the other children in his class.

Child's interests: Chess.

Title: Getting involved in my classmates' interests – Peter's story

My name is Peter. I go to St Mary's National Boy's School. Usually my teacher is Mr Lopez. There are other boys in my class too. The boys in my class are called my classmates.

There is usually free time during the school day when I can play and talk with my classmates. Lunchtime in the classroom and break in the yard are examples of free time at school. Sometimes Mr Lopez lets the class play games when it is not break time. This is also free time when I am allowed to talk to the boys in my class.

It is hard to get to know new people and to make new friends. It is hard to know what to say in conversations. Sometimes I talk about my interests like playing chess. This is okay. Sometimes the boys in my class would like to talk about their interests. This is okay too. I will try to get involved in my classmates' interests. I will try to talk to my classmates about their interests.

The perfect opportunity to get involved in my classmates' interests is during free time at school. I will try and get involved in my classmates' interests during free time.
I could get involved in my classmates' interests by talking to them about what they like. I could do this by asking them a question about their interests to start a conversation.

I could say something like 'What do you like to do?'
I could say 'What is your favourite TV show?'
I could say 'Do you do anything after school like dancing or a sport?'
I could say something else.

I will try to get involved in my classmates' interests by asking them a question about what they like. My classmates like it when I ask them questions about themselves when I am sitting or playing with them.

I could ask them 'What did you do last weekend?'

I could say 'Are you going on holiday this summer?'

I could ask my classmates 'What games do you have at home?'

I could say something else.

Asking my classmates about their interests is a good thing to do. My classmates will be happy if I express an interest in what they like and ask them questions.

I could get involved in my classmates' interests by showing them that I am listening to what they tell me. I could do this by saying something like 'That is very interesting.' I could say 'Could you tell me more about that?' I could say something else. I will try to get involved in my classmates' interests by showing them that I am listening to what they have to say. This is a good thing to do.

I will try to get involved in my classmates' interests. My classmates will be happy if I get involved in their interests.

Asking my friends questions about themselves

BACKGROUND: This story was written for Amy to improve her social communication skills. Amy was a very verbal child who talked with her classmates regularly during play. Much like the previous story, Amy liked to talk about things that interested her. Luckily for Amy, her interests were quite similar to those of her peers. Amy's conversations were very one-sided, however. She would talk at length about herself and what she thought, but never encouraged her peers to contribute to the conversation. This Social Narrative focused on including her peers more in the conversation by asking them questions about themselves.

Child's interests: Drama, Justin Bieber and Selena Gomez.

Title: Asking my friends questions about themselves – Amy's story

My name is Amy.
I go to Highland Infant School.
Usually my teacher is Ms Grogan.

Sometimes there is free time at school when I can play and talk with my friends.
Sometimes I play a game like snap.
Sometimes I talk about Justin Bieber and Selena Gomez.
Sometimes I have drama after school.

I will try to ask my friends questions about themselves during free time.

My friends like it when I ask them questions when I am sitting or playing with them.

I could say 'What are you playing with?'

I could say 'What is your favourite thing to do?'

I could say 'What type of music do you like?'

I could say 'What is your favourite TV show?'

I could ask them something else.

Talking to my friends and asking them questions about themselves is a good thing to do.

I will try to talk to my friends during free time.

I will try to listen to their answers.

I will try to listen to what my friends are saying.

My friends will be happy if I listen to them when they are talking about themselves.

I will try to ask my friends questions about themselves when they are sitting or playing with me.

My friends will be happy if I ask them questions about themselves and listen to their answers.

When I want to change topics in a conversation

BACKGROUND: This Social Narrative was written for Emily. She loved talking about her special interest, Disney cartoons, with her parents. Her parents, however, also wanted to talk to her about other topics, like how her school day went, and what she did with her after-school minder. When her parents asked her questions about her day, Emily would often ignore them in favour of talking about Disney, or would shout the responses and appear frustrated. This story was written to explain the importance of turn-taking in conversation.

Child's interests: Disney cartoons.

Title: Talking about my interests when it is my turn – Emily's story

My name is Emily.

I live with my mum and my dad in New England.

___

After school I usually talk to my mum and dad.

Sometimes I talk about Disney cartoons.

This is okay.

___

Sometimes Mum and Dad talk to me about other things.

They might want to talk to me about school or my time out with my minder, Sally.

___

I will try to talk to my Mum and Dad when they are talking to me.

I will try to talk to them politely.

I will try to answer my mum and dad when they ask me questions.

I will try to answer their questions politely.

Mum and Dad are interested in what I have to say.

After I have answered their questions I can change what we talk about.

I can change what we talk about only when Mum and Dad finish asking me their questions.

I could talk to them about the Disney movie I watched at school that day.

I could say 'What is your favourite Frozen song?'

I could ask or tell them something else.

My parents will be happy we take turns talking about what we both like.

Immature interests

BACKGROUND: This story was written for Noam. He was going to school in an integrated setting with typically developing peers. Noam loved his Barney teddy bear and would bring it to school with him to play. His classmates considered this an immature interest, and were not motivated to initiate play with him. This story was developed to encourage Noam to play with a variety of toys available to him in the classroom. This story is a good example of how a skill can be broken down into smaller steps for gradual change. The ultimate goal for Noam is to integrate more with his class and to develop friendships. Playing with a variety of toys is an important skill to develop and build on.

Child's interests: Barney the teddy bear.

Title: Playing with different toys – Noam's story

My name is Noam.
I go to Stratford National School.
Usually my teacher is Mr Smith.

Sometimes Mr Smith lets the children in the class play with toys in the classroom.
This is called playtime.

Usually I play with the Barney teddy bear.
This is okay.

It is good to play with more than one toy during playtime.
I will try to play with more than one toy during playtime.

I could play with Barney for five minutes.
I could then play with a different toy for another five minutes.

Mr Smith will tell me when to switch toys.
I will try to switch toys when Mr Smith tells me to.

I could make a jigsaw.
I could make something out of Lego® pieces.

I could read a book.
I could play with the kitchen.

I could play with the cards.
I could draw a picture with the crayons.

Mr Smith will be happy if I play with more than one toy during playtime.
I will try to switch toys during playtime.
This is a good thing to do.

Appropriate speech

Speaking in a high-pitched voice

BACKGROUND: This Social Narrative was developed for Andrew, a very emotional child, who was very sensitive to change. Andrew was regularly upset during the school day. When Andrew was upset, he would talk in a very high-pitched voice. Over time, Andrew started to use this high-pitched voice when speaking to his peers too, even if he was not apparently upset. This story was developed to help Andrew cope with his emotions and to stay calm, and to encourage him to speak in his normal voice when talking to his peers.

Child's interests: Books and cartoons.

Title: Talking nicely – Andrew's story

My name is Andrew.

I go to St Paul's School.

Usually my teacher is Miss Fahy.

_____

There is usually free time at school when I can talk to my friends.

Sometimes I talk to my friends in the yard.

Sometimes I talk to my friends in the classroom.

Sometimes I can talk to my friends when I eat my lunch.

_____

I will try to talk nicely to my friends.

I will try to talk nicely to the teachers in my school.

I will try to talk in my normal voice.

_____

Sometimes during free time I do what I like to do and read a book.
This is okay.

Sometimes I talk about what I like.
Sometimes I talk about funny cartoon clips.
I will try to talk in my normal voice.

Sometimes when I am with my friends they talk to me.
I will try to remember to talk nicely with my friends.

I will try to listen to what they have to say.
I will try to answer my friends when they ask me a question.
I will try to talk nicely.

I will try to make my friends feel good when they talk to me.
I will try to speak in my normal voice.
My friends like it when I speak in my normal voice.

Sometimes when I am with my friends or a teacher something happens to make me upset.
Sometimes someone will do something I do not like.
Sometimes I am angry.
This is okay.

I will try to stay calm.
I will try to talk nicely.

I will try to explain calmly why I am upset.
I will try to speak in my normal calm voice.
This is a good thing to do.

I will try to speak nicely to my friends and the teachers in my school.

I will try to talk nicely when something goes wrong.

I will try to say nice things to my friends and my teacher.

I will try to speak in my normal voice.

My friends and my teacher will be happy if I talk nicely.

Shouting in play

BACKGROUND: Much like the previous sample story, this Social Narrative focused on encouraging typical speech. This particular story was written for Alex who had a tendency to shout when he was excited. He would jump up and down, and emit loud short bursts of sound. This would disrupt the class at school, and disrupt his play. His peers would regularly ask him to stop shouting and cover their ears.

Child's interests: Singing.

Title: Using my quiet voice – Alex's story

My name is Alex.
I go to St Colmcilles Infant School.
Usually my teacher is Ms Mahoney.

___

There are a lot of things to do at school.
Sometimes I make music and sing songs.
Sometimes at school I talk and play with my friends.

___

Sometimes when I talk and play with my friends I get excited.
This is okay.

___

I will try to listen to my voice.
If my voice is loud I will try and make it quieter.

___

I will try and keep my voice low when I play and talk with my friends.

I will try and talk in my normal quiet voice.

I will try to talk in my normal quiet voice when I am talking with my friends.

I will try to talk in my normal quiet voice when I am playing with my friends.

I will try and talk in my normal quiet voice when I am playing on the playground.

I will try and talk in my normal quiet voice when I am playing in the classroom.

I will try to talk in my normal quiet voice when I am working in the classroom.

I will try to talk in my normal quiet voice.

This is a good thing to do.

My friends and my teacher will be happy if I talk to them in my normal quiet voice.

Preparing for a social event

Play at a birthday party

BACKGROUND: This is a different type of story from the sample stories previously presented. This Social Narrative is to prepare the child for a single event, their own birthday party. Make sure to introduce this story a few weeks in advance of the birthday party, so the child has time to learn the behaviours and be fully prepared. There is limited opportunity for the child to practice these skills before the main event. It is a good idea to use role-play to support the Social Narrative in this instance so that the child is comfortable with the behaviours on the day. This story could be adapted to prepare a child for attendance at other birthday parties. There are a number of behaviours targeted in this story, including sharing toys, playing together and the birthday cake routine. This is therefore an advanced story for a child with advanced verbal and cognitive abilities. For younger children, or children with lower verbal skills, this story would need to be divided into three shorter stories targeting each behaviour separately.

Child's interests: Trains and Mario Kart.

Title: My birthday party – Maddy's story

My name is Maddy.
My birthday is on the 1st of November every year.

Sometimes people have a party to celebrate their birthday.
This year I am having a birthday party.

The children at my birthday party are my friends.
I will try to play with my friends at my birthday party.

I will try to join in the games that mum organizes.

I could play pin the tail on the donkey.
I could play musical chairs.
I could play musical statues.

I could show my friends my toys.
I could show my friends my train collection.

I could show my friends my Wii.
We could play Mario Kart on the Wii together.

I could play something else with my friends.

After we play games we will have birthday cake.
My cake will be in the shape of a train.

Mum will light the candles on the cake.
This is okay.

I will try to blow the candles out on the cake.
I will try to wait until the birthday song is finished before I blow out the candles.

Mum will then cut up the cake.
This is okay too.
I could help mum cut up the cake.

Everyone who wants a slice of cake can have one.
I will try to share my birthday cake.

My friends will be happy if I play with them.
My friends will be happy if I share my birthday cake.

References

APA (American Psychiatric Association) (2000) *Diagnostic and Statistical Manual of Mental Disorders* (4th edn: Text revision, DSM-IV-TR). Washington, DC: APA.

Baker, M.J. (2000) 'Incorporating the thematic ritualistic behaviours of children with autism into games: increasing social play interactions with siblings.' *Journal of Positive Behaviour Interventions 2*(2), 66–84.

Baron-Cohen, S. (1988) 'Social and pragmatic deficits in autism: cognitive or affective?' *Journal of Autism and Developmental Disorders 18*(3), 379–402.

Baron-Cohen, S. (2008) *Autism and Asperger Syndrome (The Facts).* New York: Oxford University Press.

Baron-Cohen, S. and Goodhart, F. (1994) 'The 'seeing-leads-to-knowing' deficit in autism: the Pratt and Bryant probe.' *British Journal of Developmental Psychology 12*(3), 397–401.

Baron-Cohen, S., Leslie, A.M. and Frith, U. (1985) 'Does the autistic child have a 'theory of mind'?' *Cognition 21*(1), 37–46.

Baron-Cohen, S., O'Riordan, M., Stone, V., Jones, R. and Plaisted, K. (1999) 'Recognition of faux pas by normally developing children and children with Asperger syndrome or high-functioning autism.' *Journal of Autism and Developmental Disorders 29*(5), 407–418.

Bartak, L., Bottroff, V. and Zeitz, J. (2006) 'Therapist insights in working with stress in people with autism.' In M.G. Baron, J. Groden, G. Groden and L.P. Lipsitt (eds) *Stress and Coping in Autism* (pp.246–274). New York: Oxford University Press.

Beauchamp, M.H. and Anderson, V. (2010) 'SOCIAL: an integrative framework for the development of social skills.' *Psychological Bulletin 136*(1), 39–64.

Begeer, S., Malle, B.F., Nieuwland, M.S. and Keysar, B. (2010) 'Using theory of mind to represent and take part in social interactions: comparing individuals with high functioning autism and typically developing controls.' *European Journal of Developmental Assessment 7*(1), 104–122.

Booth, R. and Happé, F. (2010) '"Hunting with a knife and…fork": examining central coherence in autism, attention deficit/hyperactivity disorder, and typical development with a linguistic task.' *Journal of Experimental Child Psychology 107*(4–5), 377–393.

Boyd, B.A., Conroy, M.A., Mancil, G.R., Nakao, T. and Alter, P.J. (2007) 'Effects of circumscribed interests on the social behaviours of children with autism spectrum disorders.' *Journal of Autism and Developmental Disorders 37*(8), 1550–1561.

Boyd, B.A., McBee, M., Holtzclaw, T., Baranek, G.T. and Bodfish, J.W. (2009) 'Relationships among repetitive behaviors, sensory features, and executive functions in high functioning autism.' *Research in Autism Spectrum Disorders 3*(4), 959–966.

Burnette, C.P., Mundy, P.C., Meyer, J.A., Sutton, S.K., Vaughan, A.E. and Charak, D. (2005) 'Weak central coherence and its relations to theory of mind and anxiety in autism.' *Journal of Autism and Developmental Disorders 35*(1), 63–73.

Campbell, A. and Tincani, M. (2011) 'The power card strategy: strength-based intervention to increase direction following of children with autism spectrum disorder.' *Journal of Positive Behaviour Interventions 13*, 240–249.

Carter, A.S., Ornstein Davis, N., Klin, A. and Volker, F.R. (2005) 'Social Development in Autism.' In F.R. Volker, R. Paul, A. Klin and D. Cohen (eds) *Handbook of Autism and Pervasive Developmental Disorders* (3rd edn, Vol. One: Diagnosis, Development, Neurobiology and Behavior, pp.312–334). Hoboken, NJ: Wiley.

Centers for Disease Control and Prevention (2014) 'Prevalence of autism spectrum disorder among children aged 8 years – autism and developmental disabilities monitoring network, 11 sites, United States, 2010.' *Surveillance Summaries 63*(SS02), 1–21.

Charlop-Christy, M.H. and Haymes, L.K. (1998) 'Using objects of obsession as token reinforcers for children with autism.' *Journal of Autism and Developmental Disorders 28*(3), 189–198.

Chen, Y.-H., Rodgers, J. and McConachie, H. (2009) 'Restricted and repetitive behaviours, sensory processing and cognitive style in children with autism spectrum disorders.' *Journal of Autism and Developmental Disorders 39*, 635–642.

Coleman, R.E. (1975) 'Manipulation of self-esteem as a determinant of mood elated and depressed women.' *Journal of Abnormal Psychology 84*(6), 693–700.

Cotugno, A.J. (2009) 'Social competence and social skills training and intervention for children with autism spectrum disorders.' *Journal of Autism and Developmental Disorders 39*, 1268–1277.

Davis, K.M., Boon, R.T., Cihak, D.F. and Fore III, C. (2010) 'Power cards to improve conversational skills in adolescents with Asperger syndrome.' *Focus on Autism and Other Developmental Disabilities 25*(1), 12–22.

Desmarais, C., Roeber, B.J., Smith, M.E. and Pollak, S.D. (2012) 'Sentence comprehension in postinstitutionalised school-age children.' *Journal of Speech, Language, and Hearing Research 55*(1), 45–54.

Donnellan, A.M., Leary, M.R. and Patterson Robledo, J. (2006) 'I Can't Get Started: Stress and the Role of Movement Differences in People with Autism.' In M.G. Baron, J. Groden, G. Groden and L.P. Lipsitt (eds) *Stress and Coping in Autism* (pp.205–245). New York: Oxford University Press.

Foster, S.L. and Mash, E.J. (1999) 'Assessing social validity in clinical treatment research issues and procedures.' *Journal of Consulting and Clinical Psychology 67*(3), 308–319.

Hauck, M., Fein, D., Waterhouse, L. and Feinstein, C. (1995) 'Social initiations by autistic children to adults and other children.' *Journal of Autism and Developmental Disorders 25*, 579–595.

Henderson, H.A., Zahka, N.E., Kojkowski, N.M., Inge, A.P., Schwartz, C.B., Hileman, C.M. *et al.* (2009) 'Self-referenced memory, social cognition, and symptom presentation in autism.' *Journal of Child Psychology and Psychiatry 50*(7), 853–861.

Hughes, C., Russell, J. and Robbins, T.W. (1994) 'Evidence for executive dysfunction in autism.' *Neuropsychologia 32*(4), 477–492.

Janzen, J.E., Baron, M.G. and Groden, J. (2006) 'Understanding the Role of Stress in Autism: The Key to Teaching for Independence.' In M.G. Baron, J. Groden, G. Groden and L.P. Lipsitt (eds) *Stress and Coping in Autism* (pp.324–350). New York: Oxford University Press.

Juranek, J., Filipek, P.A., Berenji, G.R., Modahl, C., Osann, K. and Spence, M.A. (2006) 'Association between amygdala volume and anxiety level: magnetic resonance imaging (MRI) study in autistic children.' *Journal of Child Neurology 21*(12), 1051–1058.

Justice, L.M., Skibbe, L.E., McGinty, A.S., Piasta, S.B. and Petrill, S. (2011) 'Feasibility, efficacy, and social validity of home-based storybook reading intervention for children with language impairment.' *Journal of Speech, Language, and Hearing Research 54*, 523–538.

Järvinen-Pasley, A., Peppé, S., King-Smith, G. and Heaton, G. (2008) 'The relationship between form and function level receptive prosodic abilities in autism.' *Journal of Autism and Developmental Disorders 38*(7), 1328–1340.

Kana, R.K., Keller, T.A., Cherkassky, V.L., Minshew, N.J. and Just, M.A. (2006) 'Sentence comprehension in autism: thinking in pictures with decreased functional connectivity.' *Brain 129*(9), 2484–2493.

Kanner, L. (1943) 'Autistic disturbances of affective contact.' *Nervous Child 2*, 217–250.

Keeling, K., Smith Myles, B., Gagnon, E. and Simpson, R.L. (2003) 'Using the power card strategy to teach sportsmanship skills to a child with autism.' *Focus on Autism and Other Developmental Disabilities 18*(2), 103–109.

Kenworthy, L., Black, D.O., Harrison, B., della Rosa, A. and Walace, G.L. (2009) 'Are executive control functions related to autism symptoms in high functioning children?' *Child Neuropsychology 15*(5), 425–440.

Klein, S.B. (2012) 'Self, memory, and the self-reference effect: an examination of conceptual and methodological issues.' *Personality and Social Psychology Review 16*(3), 283–300.

Koegel, L.K., Koegel, R.L., Frea, W.D. and Green-Hopkins, I. (2003) 'Priming as a method of coordinating educational services for students with autism.' *Language, Speech, and Hearing Services in Schools 34*(3), 228–235.

Kokina, A. and Kern, L. (2010) 'Social Story interventions for students with autism spectrum disorders: a meta-analysis.' *Journal of Autism and Developmental Disorders 40*(7), 812–826.

LeMonda, B.C., Holtzer, R. and Goldman, S. (2012) 'Relationship between executive functions and motor stereotypies in children with autistic disorder.' *Research in Autism Spectrum Disorders 6*(3), 1099–1106.

Lind, S.E. (2010) 'Memory and the self in autism.' *Autism 14*(5), 430–456.

Lombardo, M.V., Barnes, J.L., Wheelwright, S. and Baron-Cohen, S. (2007) 'Self-referential cognition and empathy in autism.' *PLos ONE 2*, e883.

Lopez, B.R., Lincoln, A.J., Ozonoff, S. and Lai, Z. (2005) 'Examining the relationship between executive functions and restricted, repetitive symptoms of autistic disorder.' *Journal of Autism and Developmental Disorders 35*(4), 445–460.

Loth, E., Gómez, J.C. and Happé, F. (2008) 'Event schemas in autism spectrum disorders: the role of theory of mind and weak central coherence.' *Journal of Autism and Developmental Disorders 38*(3), 449–463.

McConnell, S.R. (2002) 'Interventions to facilitate social interaction for young children with autism: review of available research and recommendations for educational intervention and future research.' *Journal of Autism and Developmental Disorders 32*(5), 351–372.

Mesibov, G.B. and Howley, M. (2003) *Assessing the Curriculum for Pupils with Autistic Spectrum Disorders: Using the TEACCH Programme to Help Inclusion.* London: David Fulton.

Minshew, N.J. and Williams, D.L. (2008) 'Brain behavior connections in autism.' *Speaker's Journal 8*(5), 25–43.

Muris, P., Steerneman, P., Merckelbach, H., Holdrinet, I. and Meesters, C. (1998) 'Comorbid anxiety symptoms in children with pervasive developmental disorder.' *Journal of Anxiety Disorders 12*(4), 387–393.

O'Connor, E. (2009) 'The use of Social Story DVDs to reduce anxiety levels: a case study of a child with autism and learning disabilities.' *Support for Learning* 24(3), 133–136.

Okada, S., Ohtake, Y. and Yanagihara, M. (2010) 'Improving the manners of a student with autism: the effects of manipulating perspective holders in Social Stories – a pilot study.' *International Journal of Disability, Development and Education* 7(2), 207–219.

Ozonoff, S. (1998) 'Assessment and Remediation of Executive Dysfuntion in Autism and Asperger Syndrome.' In E. Schopler, G.B. Mesibov and L.J. Kunce (eds) *Asperger Syndrome or High-Functioning Autism?* (pp.263–292). New York: Plenum Press.

Quill, K.A. (1997) 'Instructional considerations for young children with autism: the rationale for visually cued instruction.' *Journal of Autism and Developmental Disorders* 27(6), 697–714.

Quirmbach, L.M., Lincoln, A.J., Feinberg-Gizzo, M.J., Ingersoll, B.R. and Andrews, S.M. (2009) 'Social Stories: mechanisms of effectiveness in increasing game play skills in children diagnosed with autism spectrum disorder using a pretest posttest repeated measures randomized control group design.' *Journal of Autism and Developmental Disorders* 39(2), 299–321.

Rapoff, M.A. (2010) 'Editorial: Assessing and enhancing clinical significance/social validity of intervention research in paediatric psychology.' *Journal of Paediatric Psychology* 35(2), 114–119.

Reynhout, G. and Carter, M. (2011) 'Social Stories™: A possible theoretical rationale.' European *Journal of Special Needs Education* 26(3), 367–378.

Russell, J., Mathner, N., Sharpe, S. and Tidswell, T. (1991) 'The 'Windows task' as a measure of strategic deception in preschoolers and autistic subjects.' *British Journal of Developmental Psychology* 9(2), 331–349.

Rutherford, M.D. and Rogers, S.J. (2003) 'Cognitive underpinnings of pretend play in autism.' *Journal of Autism and Developmental Disorders* 33(3), 289–302.

Sansosti, F.J. and Powell-Smith, K.A. (2008) 'Using computer-presented social stories and video models to increase the social communication skills of children with high-functioning autism spectrum disorders.' *Journal of Positive Behaviour Interventions* 10(3), 162–178.

Sayers, N., Oliver, C., Ruddick, L. and Wallis, B. (2011) 'Stereotyped behavior in children with autism and intellectual disability: an examination of the executive dysfunction hypothesis.' *Journal of Intellectual Disability Research* 55(7), 699–709.

Siegel, B., Vukicevic, J., Elliot, G.R. and Kraemer, H.C. (1989) 'The use of signal detection theory to assess the DSM-III-R criteria for autistic disorder.' *Journal of the American Academy of Child and Adolescent Psychiatry* 28(4), 542–548.

Silver, M. and Oakes, P. (2001) 'Evaluation of a new computer intervention to teach people with autism or Asperger syndrome to recognise and predict emotions in others.' *Autism* 5(3), 299–316.

Vismara, L.A. and Lyons, G.L. (2007) 'Using perseverative interests to elicit joint attention behaviours in young children with autism: theoretical and clinical implications for understanding motivation.' *Journal of Positive Behaviour Interventions* 9(4), 214–228.

West, E.A. (2008) 'Effects of verbal cues versus pictorial cues on the transfer of stimulus control for children with autism.' *Focus on Autism and Other Developmental Disabilities* 23(4), 229–241.

White, S.W., Albano, A.M., Johnson, C.R., Kasari, C., Ollendick, T., Klin, A. *et al.* (2010) 'Development of a cognitive-behavioural intervention program to treat anxiety and social deficits in teens with high-functioning autism.' *Clinical Child and Family Psychology Review 13*, 77–90.

Wood, J.J., Drahota, A., Sze, K., Har, K., Chiu, A. and Langer, D.A. (2009) 'Cognitive behavioural therapy for anxiety in children with autism spectrum disorders: a randomised, controlled trial.' *The Journal of Child Psychology and Psychiatry 50*(3), 224–234.

Further Reading

Getting Along with Others: Charts and Tips to Help You Teach Social Skills to Children and Reward Their Good Behavior
Ron Heron
1996
Boys Town Press

Available to order online, this book can be used alongside a Social Narrative to reward social behaviour. It outlines a rewarding schedule for learning new social skills, and provides example reward charts that will be visually motivating for children on the autism spectrum.

The Complete Guide to Asperger's Syndrome
Tony Attwood
2007
Jessica Kingsley Publishers

A comprehensive guide to Asperger's syndrome, or those individuals on the milder end of the autism spectrum. Provides an excellent overview of theory of mind, and the development of social skills.

From Anxiety to Meltdown
Deborah Lipsky
2011
Jessica Kingsley Publishers

Deborah Lipsky has a diagnosis of high-functioning autism. In this book, she provides a personal insight on anxiety in this population.

Index